THE DIGITAL JOURNALIST'S HANDBOOK

MARK S. LUCKIE

ISBN: 1450565603

Printed in the United States.

Illustrations: All illustrations by Mark S. Luckie unless otherwise noted. Pages 84, 85, 146, iStockPhoto. Screenshots used for illustrative purposes and do not represent an endorsement of this book or its content. All logos, images, and other insignia are property of their respective owners.

Photos: Pages 62, 129, 130, 137, iStockPhoto. Some photos used under Creative Commons license. Pg. 63 (top left), striatic; Pg. 63 (top right), antaean; Pg. 63 (bottom), Badboy of Maths; Pg. 65, oksidor; Pg. 69, Phil Scoville; Pg. 70, David Paul Ohmer; Pg. 113, moonlightbulb; Pg. 119, Nicholas_T; Pg. 198, james.thompson; Pg. 131, JerryFeist; Pg. 213, puliarf. Author photo: Fernando Aguila.

CONTENTS

ACKNOWLEDGEMENTS

To my family: Mom, Aerick, Arianna, and Amani, and to the bumpers to my pinball: Melissa June, Kimberley Jace, Paul Grabowicz, Lanita Pace-Hinton, @RandomtoReason, and the NYC rooftop crew.

Dedicated to the journalists of the world who are just trying to tell stories the best way they know how.

THE NEW MEDIA MINDSET

CHAPTER ONE

If you're looking for an apocalyptic dissertation on why journalism is dying, this isn't the book for you. *The Digital Journalist's Handbook* is your guide to the tools you need to know to thrive in today's digital newsroom.

As recently as a few years ago, the word "journalism" referred to newspaper and magazine stories or television and radio broadcasts. Now, the definition of journalism has expanded to include news stories published on the web. As computers become cheaper and internet connection speeds become faster, the number of people who look to the internet as a primary source of news is growing. The internet has surpassed all other media, except television, as a source of news and many readers look to the web for updates on national and international news stories, according to a study by the Pew Research Center. Nearly every major news organization has an online presence that accompanies its traditional publication. Often, online news sites draw many more millions of readers and viewers than their print or broadcast counterparts. Now more than ever, it is important for reporters, editors, and everyone at every stage of the news cycle to be familiar with the technologies that are shaping online journalism.

Unlike radio, which can only air audio, and television, which can only provide video, the internet can be a platform for all the previously mentioned media. Audiences can watch or listen to traditional radio and television broadcasts on the web and print stories and other visual elements such as graphics and photographs are regularly published online. Journalists can also use the internet as a tool to combine previously separate media to tell a single story. For example, text stories posted online are sometimes accompanied by video clips and online audio stories can be paired with text and images. Also, audiences no longer have to sit in front of a television or spend an hour flipping through a newspaper to find the news that matters to them. Anyone can log on to the internet to instantly access the news they want and read or view it whenever they choose, even if it is days or weeks later.

The new era of journalism has many names including "digital journalism," "multimedia journalism," "interactive journalism," and "new media," each of which has slightly different definitions, but all of which refer to the use of digital technology, computers, and the internet to enhance traditional storytelling. "New media" commonly refers to newer forms of journalism that have emerged since the inception of online news. However, the term has itself become outdated as digital tools and online technology are a standard and permanent presence in newsrooms everywhere.

"Multimedia journalism" is a term that describes online stories that blend text, photos, audio, video and/or graphics into a single story or project. For example, audio slideshows (outlined in Chapter 6) combine photos, audio recordings, and text to tell a news story using various media. A multimedia story often appeals to many kinds of readers because it communicates the news with various media that each draw the reader into the story. "Interactive journalism" can refer to either online stories that respond to input from the reader or the interaction made possible by online tools like social networks and wikis. Social networks, online communities where users communicate and interact with each other, and wikis, tools that allow online users to collaboratively author, edit, and modify information, allow web users to interact with news stories, newsroom staff, and each other.

Before the web and online communities became an integral part of journalism, relatively small groups of editors and reporters selected the news stories that were covered and dictated the news of the day to the rest of the world. However, traditional media are no longer the only sources of news. The web has empowered anyone with a computer to report their own news stories and share them with friends and family or a global audience. Citizen journalists, ordinary citizens without formal training and no affiliation with a traditional news outlet, are using blogs and other online platforms to report the news that is important to them. Independent, online-only news sites and bloggers often work outside the traditional channels of journalism and cover local, national, and international news. The internet has transformed journalism from a one-way dialogue between traditional media and an audience to a marketplace of ideas where the audience no longer has to rely on traditional media to receive the news.

The rise in citizen journalism is due in part to the decreasing cost of digital media tools and the increasing use of the web as a platform for self-publishing. In the past, news audiences had to wait for the reporter to arrive at the scene to be notified of breaking news. Today, news is more often relayed by witnesses already at the scene who post news happening around them to social networks and blogs using tools they already have on hand. These tools include cell phones enabled with text messaging, email, and photo or video capabilities. There is still a difference between a credentialed reporter and a casual, yet well-equipped observer who reports what they see, but that line has become increasingly blurred. Some citizen journalists and bloggers may lack the formal editorial processes that journalists must follow, but they are no less important to journalism and the distribution of news.

The web doesn't spell an end to journalism — it has only changed the way news is delivered. The internet can extend the reach of a print publication or broadcast and news is no longer confined to a physical or geographic location. Stories that were once viewable only by those with access to a local broadcast station or newspaper can now be seen around the world. For example, a student in Texas can easily read the latest news from Shanghai just by accessing the web.

The internet has not only affected how news is distributed, but the structure of traditional newsrooms as well. When online news was in its infancy, the web staff was usually one or two people in a corner of the newsroom. As media companies' web presence grew, so did the staff, yet online staff and news reporters often remained in separate areas of the newsroom, sometimes on different floors or even in different buildings. Now that the number of online readers is increasing and many more people turn to the web for news, many media companies have integrated the web staff into the newsroom and online producers often share the same space as traditional print and broadcast news reporters. Reporters are also tackling duties that used to be handed off to web producers, including posting their stories and creating multimedia content.

No two news websites are alike and there are various media with an online presence, including newspapers, magazines, local and cable television networks, radio stations and syndicated programs, and online-only news outlets. Each media and each newsroom has its own unique approach to online news. However, they do share a common bond — a commitment to using the web and digital media tools to tell stories and enhance the way news is delivered.

The new era of journalism requires journalists to adopt new skills in addition to reporting and writing. Multimedia journalists are trained in photography, videography, audio recording, web and graphic design, programming, or any combination of these, and use these diverse skills to enhance their reporting. Many reporters are now *backpack journalists* or *mojos* (short for "mobile journalists"), and use laptops, mobile phones, and digital tools to report from remote locations far away from the newsroom. In the past, news stories were written by one or two reporters. Now, multimedia projects are often created by teams of journalists with different skills who together produce interactive and multimedia news projects. A multimedia journalist must not only know how to use digital tools, but also have the wisdom to know which medium is right for a particular news story.

Traditional journalism and digital or "new media" journalism are not that dissimilar — both require basic reporting skills. This book assumes you are familiar with the fundamentals of journalism, including how to write (well), interview, establish trust and relationships, and how to report facts and information. Digital tools simply build on these skills and incorporate technology into traditional storytelling.

Not everyone who is open to learning digital media technologies will have the aptitude to use them. Digital journalism requires creativity as well as technical skills that don't often come naturally to writers or journalists. The transition from traditional to digital journalist takes time and cannot be forced on anyone who isn't ready to adapt. By reading this book, you have shown a commitment to the advancement of journalism and your own reporting.

The Digital Journalist's Handbook outlines the features and functions of various digital tools and provides guidelines on how journalists can use them. After reading this book, it is up to you to decide which technologies you will explore further and incorporate into your work. As a supplement to this book, you can find in-depth, step-by-step instructions on specific programs or equipment at *The Handbook* website (*www.djhandbook.net*). When you see the globe icon, visit the listed web address for additional resources, tutorials, and examples of the tools discussed in that section. You can also visit 10,000 Words (*www.10000words. net*), the blog on which this book is based, for continued resources and tutorials.

Good luck. The future of journalism is in your hands.

WRITING FOR THE WEB

CHAPTER TWO

Journalism has existed for centuries, long before the computer, the typewriter, and even the reporter's notepad. In that time, journalists frequently accented their writing with clever ledes, lengthy anecdotes, and elaborate words that required a dictionary to understand. The web has brought much of this complex writing to a halt. As print stories move from paper to the web, journalism has given way to brevity and readability to make stories more accessible and easier to understand. Several studies of how people interact with the web show that online audiences want to read the news quickly and instantly understand the point of a story. Many online readers are scanning instead of reading stories, looking for words and sentences that quickly identify the key points and issues. Instead of reading whole paragraphs, readers scan for brief bits of text like headlines, article summaries, and captions, according to a study by Stanford University and the Poynter Institute. Because online audiences often lack the patience to read lengthy or elaborate articles, news stories written for the web should be concise and include only the information necessary to tell the story.

The best online writing follows the "inverted pyramid" structure, a technique long used in print journalism where the most important and interesting information appears at the top of the story in the very first paragraphs. Details, quotes, and further information and analysis appear in the following paragraphs, arranged in order of importance. This style of writing, so named because the pattern is similar to an upside-down pyramid, allows readers to stop reading the story at any point and still understand the main topic and issues, even if they haven't read all the details. Also, the wordy anecdotes that lead many traditional newspaper and magazine stories should be moved from the top few paragraphs to later in the story after the most important information is presented. If you do not follow this model and instead place critical information lower in the story, an online reader is less likely to see it.

To help readers better scan an online story, paragraphs should be formatted so they are relatively short and include no more than two to three sentences. Each paragraph should contain a single idea and that idea should be presented at the beginning of the block of text. This way, the reader who is scanning the story will understand the content of the paragraph even if they don't read the entire text. Online readers scan the first sentence or two of each paragraph and may miss additional information if it appears further in the paragraph, according to the Stanford/Poynter study. Larger paragraphs create unscannable blocks of text that the reader cannot quickly understand. Breaking up the text allows the reader to better absorb the information contained in an online news story.

The challenge of making online text easier to read extends to the text itself. Along with creating shorter blocks of text, writing for the web requires journalists to use fewer words to make their point. For example, complex sentences like "The harried and haggard woman trudged to the shopping center, one heavy foot in front of the other" could be written as "The woman walked slowly to the market," reducing the amount of reading necessary to understand the point of the text. Also, using large words may not bother more educated readers, but others may be thrown off by words they don't immediately understand. The reading level of the average internet user is lower than the average journalist, so while an elaborate vocabulary may impress more learned readers, others will be left searching for a dictionary. Instead, use short, familiar words that don't require the reader to spend additional time considering the meaning of the word. You can also improve your writing by removing unnecessary pieces of information. If a specific fact or opinion is repeated several times in a story, make the point once and reduce the amount of time required to read the text.

Most news sites include a dateline above online stories that indicates when the article was written. Online stories, however, may be read weeks, months, or even years after they are first written. Online readers sometimes skip the dateline and instead begin reading at the first paragraph. To eliminate possible confusion, avoid including nonspecific time markers such as "last night" or "tomorrow" in your writing and instead use dates like "Friday" or the day and the month (e.g. "October 1").

The web does not have the same time or space restrictions that limit the length of traditional print or broadcast stories, but there is a limit to how much text the average online visitor will read before they click away. Lengthy stories can be broken up over several individual web pages, a technique called *pagination*. Pagination is the process of dividing online content such as news stories into chunks and displaying it on separate pages that the reader can click through. The formatting breaks up lengthy stories and the monotony of scrolling through seemingly endless blocks of text. Paginated articles include a navigation system at the bottom of the page that contains links the reader can click to read more of the story. This navigation can take several forms, including numbers, arrows, or "previous" and "next" links and can be created manually or automatically, depending on the architecture of the website.

Go to page: 1 2 3 4 5 [Next ▸]		First « Previous Page 4 of 10 Next » Last
Page 1│2│3│4│5 Next Page		« Previous │1│2│3│4│5│6│7│8│9│ Next »

Examples of navigation used to paginate online content

Pages should be split at natural breaks in the story, usually at cliffhangers or natural pauses. This keeps readers interested in what will happen next and encourages them to continue reading when they arrive at the end of the page. More often, pagination is used as a strategy to increase the number of *page views*, or the number of times the web page is accessed. For example, a single online article that is not paginated and is viewed 100 times will receive 100 page views. If the same story is split into three separate pages and each page is viewed 100 times, the article receives 300 page views. The amount of money a website charges its advertisers depends on the number of page views the site receives. More page views translates into higher revenue for the site.

Pagination, however, should not be abused. For example, a 500-word story distributed over five pages will likely annoy the reader who must click several times to read a brief article. Use pagination wisely because there is a limit to what readers will tolerate. Despite the popularity of pagination among online news sites, some readers prefer scrolling through a story instead of clicking through several pages. If the content is compelling, readers will continue to scroll through an article, even if it is lengthy. Some sites cater to both types of readers and offer the option to read the content of a paginated article on a single page. Your approach to making your text easier to read, whether it is pagination, formatting, or altering the text itself, should depend on the style of your newsroom.

Search engine optimization

Search engines, the online tools used to find content on the web, play a major role in how many internet users discover and access online content, including online stories produced by news websites. Search engines like Google and Yahoo Search are responsible for a large percentage of traffic to news and media sites. This online traffic often includes internet users who may not otherwise visit a news site directly.

Search engines run automated programs called *bots* or *spiders* that "crawl" billions of websites and pages and index them in a database. When a person enters a word or phrase in the search box, the search engine returns sites or online articles that contain those words. For example, if someone searches for "journalism" in Google, they are presented with a list of several million results that includes links to web pages, blogs, online articles, and more, as in the example below.

Search engine optimization, more commonly known as *SEO*, is the process of enhancing a website and its content to increase its rank in search engines. The higher a site is ranked in a search engine, the higher it appears in the results, making it more likely that potential readers and viewers will find and click on the site. For example, if your site includes several stories about cars and is ranked high by the search engine, potential readers searching for "cars" will find your site at the top of the search engine's results. Years ago, search engine users often clicked through several pages of search results to find what they were looking for. Now, many will not look past the top few results.

There are a few key strategies that can increase the probability that your story or content will be indexed by and ranked high in search engines. One of the easiest ways to optimize stories for search engines is to include *keywords* in the text and headline of online articles. Keywords are words or short phrases that represent the topic or key points of the content and are often people, places, and things. Keywords help search engines identify the content of a site and present appropriate results to people using the tool. For example, if this book was an online article, the keywords would be "The Digital Journalist's Handbook," "journalism," "technology," "multimedia," and "Mark S. Luckie." If a web user searched for these keywords in a search engine, links to the website for this book and other sites on which this book is mentioned would appear in the results.

Journalists naturally include keywords in their writing simply by identifying the subject, issues, or key players related to a story. Search engine optimization just means doing this more actively and deliberately. Writers should also include as many variations of keywords as possible in their story. For example, if a story is about journalism, but only includes the words "writing" and "reporting," a search engine user searching for the word "journalism" will likely not find the article. This doesn't mean you should stuff your writing with keywords and synonyms — keywords should be blended as naturally as possible.

When writing about a person, always include their full name and title or other identifier. For example, "ABC Company President John Johnson" is better than "President Johnson" which is not specific and will make the article more difficult to find in a search engine. In addition, avoid shortened names or nicknames on first reference (e.g. "MSU" instead of "Michigan State University" or "United" instead of "Manchester United"). This helps differentiate the subject of your article from other subjects with similar names. For example, "United" can also refer to "United Airlines" or "United Nations." This technique does not apply to commonly accepted abbreviations such as NASA, UCLA, or NATO for which search engine users are less likely to spell out the full name. The best approach to keyword integration is to think of what someone is more likely to search for. By including keywords in your story, you will make it more likely that online visitors will find your content.

Headlines

Once the search engine finds your story, site, or content, it is up to the headline to entice the potential reader to click and read more. Web headlines must be attention-grabbing, descriptive, and include important keywords, all within the span of a few words. A web headline should accurately summarize what the audience will read and be captivating enough to make them want to read it.

In the past, newsrooms often employed several copy editors to create intriguing headlines and reporters only had to worry about writing the story. Now, reporters are frequently required to create or pitch headlines to accompany their stories. The trick to writing a good headline is to think about the story and verbalize aloud what the main points of the story are. How would you describe the story to a friend who had never heard or read it before? The first things you say are often what should be included in the headline. Examine your story and identify the main subject and the keywords and phrases that should be included in the headline.

Incorporating keywords into web headlines also means eliminating the long-standing journalism tradition of including puns or other vague references to the subject in the headline of the story. The *New York Post*, for example, is famous for including clever puns on its front page headlines such as "Down and Outed in Beverly Hills" (a story about the arrest of singer George Michael in a Beverly Hills bathroom), but this type of headline does not work as well on the web. Headlines are indexed by computers that do not recognize puns. In addition, the puns may be clever, but online visitors often don't want to spend time figuring out what they mean or guess at the subject of the story. Readers want to know exactly what the story is about and often make a split-second decision whether they will read it or not. Even very short, attention-grabbing headlines are being used less frequently in favor of more search engine-friendly headers.

Today, *The (UK) Sun*'s classic headline "FREDDIE STARR ATE MY HAMSTER" would more likely be "Cheshire woman accuses comedian Freddie Starr of eating her hamster," which is more descriptive and incorporates keywords. Another classic headline, "MAN WALKS ON MOON," variations of which appeared in many major newspapers to commemorate the 1969 U.S. moon landing, would now become "U.S. astronaut Neil Armstrong becomes first man to walk on moon." This is not to say that clever headlines cannot or aren't still being used, but such headlines sacrifice potential readers.

In addition to people and search engines, headlines must also cater to *social networks*, online communities where users communicate and interact with each other and share online content. Often, news stories posted on social networks are simply a headline and a link to click for more information. There is often no context or summary that social networkers can use to judge whether they want to read the story or not, so the headline must entice them to click and read the full article. Sometimes social network users discard the original headline and create their own — one they think will better sell the story — and often pick up on an angle of the story that is important to them. For example, the headline for an article entitled "10 News photos that took retouching too far" was retitled and circulated by social network users as "10 'naughty' news photos," "Photoshopping taken too far by some photojournalists," "When Photoshop skills strike back," and "Is Photoshop evil?" The new headlines may border on provocative, but are no less relevant than the original headline.

Headlines for online news stories should be interesting enough to capture the attention of the reader, but should not oversell the content. They should still be factual, clear, and follow newsroom standards and guidelines.

The *subhead*, another carryover from traditional print journalism, is a word, phrase, or sentence fragment included in the text to describe various sections of the story. Subheads are used to break up long blocks of text and encourage the reader to continue reading. Subheads often include keywords that indicate the subject of the following paragraphs. There are several subheads in this book — "Search engine optimization" and "Headlines" which appear above sections in this chapter are similar to the subheads found in online news stories. Subheads that appear online are usually formatted as bold text or in a larger text size so they differ visually differ from the rest of the text.

Some news sites also include a summary paragraph at the beginning of online articles or content to let visitors know what they are about to read. Summaries are usually a sentence or two that describes the topic or idea of the story and helps readers decide if they want to read the full article. Multimedia content like audio, video, and multimedia files should always be accompanied by a summary paragraph that describes the content. The text of the summary is often what is indexed by search engines and appears in search results. Search engines can tell a potential reader that an audio or video file appears on the page, but they cannot tell what the video or audio contains unless a summary is also included on the page.

While it would seem like search engine optimization takes the creativity and individuality out of writing, it is actually important that each story still have voice and personality. Though search engines help people find online content, it is humans who actually read the stories and the content should still be written for them. No matter how optimized a story is for search engines, if the story or article is bad or poorly written, people will not read it. The goal of search engine optimization is not to change your writing, only to ensure as many people as possible read it. After all, that is the fundamental goal of journalism — to spread the news to as many people as possible.

Linking

One of the great advantages of online journalism is the ability to use *hyperlinks* to direct readers to additional information elsewhere on the web. Hyperlinks or *links* are a string of HTML code added to a word or group of words that when clicked, directs the user to another web page or site. Links can direct the visitor to another page on the same site or to a completely different site on the web. Links can take various forms depending on the design of the website, but are often distinguished from plain text using color, bold formatting, or an underline.

<u>Click here</u> to visit the site   The new report is **available online**.

Links are used to direct online readers to other content they may find useful or more detailed information available elsewhere on the web. In online journalism, links are used as attribution or to point readers to previously written stories. For example, if you quote a person in your story and the full statement is available online, you can use a link to indicate where the quote came from. Or, if you cite a study and the full study exists online, you can link to it so readers can explore the study for themselves. For ongoing stories, links to earlier stories should be included within or adjacent to the article because some visitors may not have read the stories that preceded it or know the history of the issue. These links often appear at the end of the story or where they can be easily be located. Most importantly, links should be useful and provide additional information or services that cannot be found on the page the visitor is reading. For example, if a story mentions that tickets for a local play are on sale, a link should be included somewhere in the story to a site where the reader can purchase tickets for the play. If such a link is not included, the reader must leave the site to search the web for tickets — time that can be spent reading more content on your site.

There are two common approaches to linking text. The first approach is to use the words "click here" or some similar variation to indicate a link. Creating a link that says "click here" makes it very obvious that the text is a link. More often, however, links are anchored to a short amount of text, usually names, keywords, or phrases that describe the content of the link and give the reader an indication of the site they will be directed to. Linking whole sentences or paragraphs of text is not descriptive and can be distracting. Links should be descriptive enough to tell the reader exactly what they are going to see if they click on the link. Whenever possible, link to the specific web page where the information can be found instead of the main site so the reader doesn't have to search for the information after clicking the link (e.g. "http://www.site.com/ site/link.html" instead of "www.site.com"). You should only link to credible sources and verify that the linked site contains factual information and appropriate content. Links are like quotes and you wouldn't quote anyone you didn't find credible.

Some news sites have policies that forbid staff from linking to any site other than its own. Such policies are meant to discourage visitors from leaving the site. Nowadays, professional news sites look behind the times if they don't include relevant links when they should obviously be included in the story. If you continue to provide good content, your readers will return to your site, even if you send them away using a link. Online readers will not click every link, just the ones they find useful and it is up to the reporter or web producer to decide which links best serve the reader.

Breaking news

When online journalism was in its infancy, many newspapers refused to post news stories to the web before they first appeared in print. Their reasoning was they didn't want to scoop themselves, or worse, allow the competition to read an online story and possibly repackage and report it for themselves. While this was a valid concern, the rationale overlooked a very important point: many readers no longer read the physical print product and instead get their news solely from online news sites. Holding stories for print is no longer a practical strategy because if stories are posted online hours later, they are already old news, both in print and on the web. Instead of being scooped in print you can also be scooped on the web where readers have several avenues to receive the latest news, often within minutes or hours after it happens.

News media are no longer competing with other newspapers, television, or radio stations to be the first to report breaking news. They are also competing with social networks, blogs, and online-only news sites that didn't exist years ago. News often circulates on blogs and social networks long before it is reported by mainstream media. For example, in January 2009, U.S. Airways Flight 1549 crash-landed in the Hudson River shortly after taking off from New York's LaGuardia airport. Janis Kruns, a member of the social network Twitter (*www.twitter.com*), was on a rescue ferry aiding the downed plane and posted photos of the crash to the website. News of the crash circulated on the internet shortly after and the photo was widely distributed minutes after it was posted. Mainstream media news outlets began reporting the crash not too long after, but had been scooped by an ordinary citizen with an internet-enabled camera phone.

In the digital age, many news readers and viewers turn to the web immediately after an event happens, so newsrooms should aim to post news online as soon as it breaks and is fact-checked. Even if a story has not fully materialized, it is important to post at least some basic information so those searching online for recent updates have at least something to read. As details emerge, the story can be updated both online and for a later publication or broadcast with additional information, quotes, or sources. In addition to a dateline, many news sites feature a time stamp on online stories that indicates when the last update was made to a particular story. This helps online readers verify that they are reading the most up-to-date information.

Even if there is a rush to post content online, it is important that each news story is reviewed by an editor or copy editor before it is posted. A major difference between traditional print and broadcast media and online stories is that corrections can easily be made to online copy immediately or long after it is first published.

However, the ability to make corrections does not give journalists a cushion when publishing online stories. Inaccurate information can circulate widely on the web before the correction is posted. Therefore, it is best to publish correct information when a story is first posted, instead of trying to backtrack later. Some online news sites like *The Wall Street Journal* (*online.wsj.com*) publish corrections at the top of the story so readers immediately know if something has changed.

While timing is a factor with online news, so is accuracy. The difference between news sites and social networks is readers still rely on factual information that is verified by a trusted news source. Online readers also depend on professional news media to provide background and context for a story. Bloggers themselves often use professional online news media as a source, linking to stories or using them as a basis for reporting or discussion. For many journalism purists, it is easy to feel threatened by other, less mainstream news sources like blogs and social networks, or even online-only news media. These sites, however, should not be seen as competition, but as a player along traditional channels of journalism.

Comments

Writing for journalism is no longer just about writing — it's also about interacting directly with your audience. In the golden days of journalism, newsroom staff reported the news without a real expectation of feedback. The only way for readers to have their say in print was to write a letter to the editor, which was then selected from a pile of other letters, edited for length, and published in a future issue. In radio, listeners are sometimes invited to call in, but are again screened and selected from a larger group of callers. This type of discussion is referred to as a "one-to-many" conversation, in that one person dictates the news and the audience — or the "many" — receives the news with few ways to reply or discuss it in a similarly public forum. The internet has introduced the "many-to-many" conversation, in which the audience can share their thoughts or contribute to a story, either on their own site or blog or adjacent to the original story.

Public discussion on online news sites usually happens in the *comment section*, a space at the end of a news article or other online content where readers can post public remarks. Comment sections are a way for audiences to share their opinion and discuss news in a public space.

Comments (3)

Don Davis | February 25, 12:13 p.m.

Maria Lopez | February 25, 12:17 p.m.

Alex Williams | February 25, 1:18 p.m.

Add Your Comment

| Submit | | Clear |

A typical comment section

Sometimes, online articles can attract comments from readers who are more knowledgeable about the subject or have related personal stories to share, which can inform both other readers and the news staff. In addition to a comment, readers can include their real name or an alias or, on some sites, post anonymously. Comments are usually not restricted in length and are displayed one after the other, usually in chronological order. All the comments on a single article can appear together on a single web page or span multiple pages, depending on the site.

Comments can also be posted in reverse chronological order with the most recent comment appearing at the top. This is a great system for viewing the most recent comments posted to an online article, but can be jarring for a reader who wants to read the comments from beginning to end. Comments are often linear discussions in which people reply to each other. If the comments are presented in reverse order, the reader must scroll to the bottom of the page and read up to follow the conversation, which is contrary to the natural way most people read online content.

Some news sites also host online *forums*, or online discussion sites, where users are invited to comment on any number of topics. Forums contain *threads* dedicated to specific topics created by site administrators or forum participants. Online comment sections are usually associated with a specific story or article, but forums are usually not limited to the stories that are presented on a particular site.

Reporters can interact with readers by joining the conversation and responding to comments. Journalists commenting on their own stories should identify themselves by name with a special note that indicates they are staff of the publication. Reporters should respond to comments to generate discussion, but should not come off as defensive. Some media companies do not allow reporters to comment on the website, so check with your supervisor to be sure. Ideally, reporters or editors should read the comments of every news story for possible leads or developments that were not included in the initial version of the story. Some news media also incorporate comments in later stories or select the best online comments and publish them in print or on air. A few news sites like *The New York Times* and The Huffington Post select the best comments and feature them on the site. Featuring notable comments gives readers an incentive to post quality or insightful remarks.

More often, comments are read by newsroom staff for *moderation* or to review or police the comment section for inflammatory, libelous, racist, sexist,

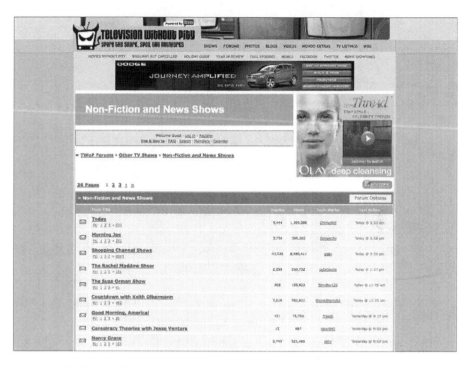

Television Without Pity (www.televisionwithoutpity.com), an online forum

homophobic, or off-topic comments. Moderators usually delete offending comments and sometimes ban recurring offenders who repeatedly post comments that negatively contribute to the online discussion. Such users are called *trolls*, online contributors who intentionally antagonize other commenters. Trolls deliberately stir up fights by posting controversial statements or simply display distasteful behavior. Another type of commenter news sites must contend with is the *spammer*, a user who includes unrelated links to their own site in their comment as a form of guerrilla advertising. Spammers often write nonsensical comments or no comment at all and simply include links to their own content. Spammers differ from commenters who may innocently include links to their own sites because they often link to sites that have nothing to do with the content. For example, many spammers post links to online pharmaceutical vendors and questionable watch and jewelry retailers. Another commonly recurring problem in online news comment sections is the *flame war*, a hostile argument between two or more commenters that distracts from the discussion.

Offensive comments are a problem everywhere on the internet, not just on news websites. In the early days of the web, many news sites were reluctant to monitor or delete such comments for fear that the news organization might be held liable for all comments left on the site. Now, some do so actively, removing inflammatory or offensive comments and the users who post them.

The extent of comment moderation is up to the individual news site. Some sites have clear rules about what comments will and won't be tolerated and have several ways of moderating or deleting offensive comments or commenters. On some sites, each comment is reviewed by a staff member before it is posted to the site. Under this system, every comment that is posted to the site is first made available in an online list or e-mailed to the site manager(s), who can decide whether to publish each comment. This process can stop offensive comments from ever appearing on the site, but it also reduces the immediacy of posting comments or replies and can stifle the conversation.

Some sites require each visitor to register with the site before they can post a comment. An online registration form often requires information such as a *username*, a unique online alias, a password, and a confirmable e-mail address. Some forms also ask visitors to submit their real names instead of a username or sign in with a social network account (see Chapter 9) to make commenters feel more responsible for their remarks. Registration has its advantages and disadvantages: on one hand, readers often don't want to or don't have time to register for a site that they may only visit once or twice. On the other hand, if a reader has a strong desire to leave a comment and join the online discussion, they will take the time to register. Those who do register are often loyal readers who are more likely to have ongoing discussions and a presence on the site. To increase the probability that the registration is completed, the form must be short. Some online sites ask for additional information like year of birth and household income that may give better insight into who the reader is, but it also increases the time necessary to post a comment to the site for the first time. There is also no guarantee that the answers submitted will be accurate.

There are many other forms of comment moderation. Some sites post a link where readers can report offensive comments or abuse. Other sites allow readers to rate comments — comments that are rated low are often considered for deletion. Many news sites also install a foul language filter that automatically detects curse words and deletes them or replaces them with asterisks or dashes. The comment section on an individual story can also be deactivated entirely by a system administrator.

There is no perfect solution to moderating comments. News media give up a little bit of control by letting readers participate in online discussions surrounding their content. The moderator or reporter may not necessarily agree with each comment, but dissent is not a reason to delete or censor a comment. In spite of the obvious flaws of the comment section, it is an invaluable tool in online news and provides a space for readers and viewers to generate a conversation around stories. At its best, the comment section is a forum for free speech and open discussion.

Analytics

For decades, newspaper reporters, and to a lesser extent broadcast journalists, performed their duties without a real idea of how many people read, watched, or listened to their stories. In the digital age, newsrooms know much more about their audience, including how many have viewed each story, because of *analytics*, the study of the behavior of website visitors. To measure analytics, newsrooms install a program or online tool that gathers data about how the site and its individual pages are accessed. Analytics tools can show how many people accessed a particular story or article, how each web visitor found the site or content, what site or page they viewed before coming to the site, and how long they stayed on the page. Analytics can also indicate what keywords people are searching for on a site and, if the visitor found the site using a *search engine*, what keywords they used to discover the content. This information helps newsroom staff learn what topics are most popular among their audience and to more accurately tailor stories to their reading habits. For example, if analytics show that stories about dogs are popular among your readers, you may consider adding more stories about dogs.

Analytics can also be a double-edged sword. On one hand it is great to learn what stories are most popular, which can in turn create a sense of achievement for the reporter or staff. On the other hand, online news stories that become popular may not be what the newsroom considers their best work. For example, it is not unheard of for celebrity news and offbeat stories to dominate the list of most viewed stories on news sites.

Newsrooms have varying policies on who has access to the site's analytics and tracking tools. Sometimes editors or news managers are the only staff to have access to the information and can choose whether to share it with the rest of their staff.

Computer-assisted reporting

The internet and other technologies have also introduced new ways to research and report news stories. Instead of physically digging through paper records and files, journalists can also use computers and online databases to conduct research and make the news-gathering process faster and easier. For example, some police dockets that once required a trip to the nearest station and were available only in print are now available online. Legal briefs and courtroom records are regularly scanned into online databases that are just a click away. Finding out more about a person or subject is as easy as entering their name into a search engine such as Google. While googling the subjects of your story is encouraged (after all the internet is one huge digital library), journalists should use caution when quoting or sourcing facts found online. Anyone can write what they want and post it to the web — and along with factual information — a lot of inaccurate, biased, or incorrect information can also be found on the web. Journalists should verify that the site or author is a trusted source. Journalists should be wary of sites with no listed author, misspelled words, or bad grammar.

Even if a site seems reliable, you should also check for a dateline to make sure the information is up to date. For example, in 2009, a *Los Angeles Times* story that indicated the California Supreme Court had overturned Proposition 8, a controversial piece of legislation that banned same-sex marriage, circulated on the social networking site Twitter, which led to heated discussion on both sides. The story that was used as evidence of the reversal was actually from nearly a year earlier, according to its dateline, and the proposition had not, in fact, been overturned.

Nothing represents the good and the bad of computer-assisted reporting like Wikipedia (*www.wikipedia.org*), an online encyclopedia and *wiki* where entries are created and updated by anyone with an internet-enabled computer. Wikipedia is one of the most visited sites on the internet and its millions of articles are consistently updated with factual, relevant information that can contribute to traditional news reporting. It is also editable by anyone, meaning everything that appears on the site may not be accurate.

Wikipedia (www.wikipedia.org)

Wikipedia has millions of contributors and a small percentage of visitors deliberately insert false information into the site's various articles. For example, in May 2009, then 22-year-old Shane Fitzgerald, a student at University College Dublin in Ireland, posted a fictitious quote to the Wikipedia entry for then recently deceased French composer Maurice Jarre. The following quote was posted to the site:

> "One could say my life itself has been one long soundtrack. Music was my life, music brought me to life, and music is how I will be remembered long after I leave this life. When I die there will be a final waltz playing in my head, that only I can hear."

Jarre never actually said the quote, yet it was included in obituaries published in several mainstream newspapers by reporters who copied it from Wikipedia, but had not actually fact-checked its origin. After the quote was exposed as a fake, several publications made corrections and retractions, but the quote still remained on several news sites and blogs.

Because such incidents occur, Wikipedia is often written off by many journalists as a source of inaccurate information. In some cases this may be true, but the site should not be discounted altogether. Often, breaking news is first posted on Wikipedia as users make up-to-the-minute updates to entries. The 2007 death of model and entertainer Anna Nicole Smith, for example, was first announced on Wikipedia, with traditional news media following shortly after. Like other online sources, information found on Wikipedia should be sourced and confirmed before it is reported by any credible news outlet. Thankfully, Wikipedia makes it easy to source information found on its pages. Like a traditional academic journal, most facts that appear on the site have a number next to them that corresponds to a link to the original on or offline article being cited. The sources listed at the bottom of each Wikipedia entry make it easier to verify that the information was first published by a credible source.

Wikipedia has many rules in place to ensure that the information that appears on the site is as credible as possible. Information posted to the site must be both neutral and come from an original published source. The Wikipedia community is great at eventually rooting out and correcting false or biased information posted on the site. Articles that are biased or lack sources are often labeled as such. Even with these measures in place, juicy tidbits found on Wikipedia or any other online site should be fact-checked and confirmed by a credible source.

Wikipedia is also an example of *crowdsourcing*, or harnessing the collective knowledge of internet users to better inform writing and reporting. Crowdsourcing is a descendant of the traditional news tip line, where readers or viewers are encouraged to call a number and report news happening near them. The news audience collectively knows more than the reporter and crowdsourcing is a great way to collect multiple viewpoints that may otherwise go unheard.

There are many ways to use the internet for crowdsourcing. One way is to ask online readers for their input on an upcoming story or idea and provide the reporter's e-mail address. Newsrooms can also use online technology to facilitate crowdsourcing on a grander scale. For example, in 2009, *The (UK) Guardian* appealed for help in sifting through more than 450,000 pages of data on government officials' expenses. The paper posted all the expense claims online (*http://mps-expenses.guardian.co.uk*) and let readers dig through them to see what they could find. Readers found lots of interesting tidbits that a small group of reporters would not have had the time to uncover themselves. From the tips, professional journalists then did additional reporting, which resulted in a series of stories based on the reports. Some news sites provide an ongoing forum for readers to contribute information and reports. For example, CNN established iReport (*www.ireport.com*) in 2008, a site that encourages citizen journalists to submit photos, video, and stories online. Some of the reports and media are broadcast on-air and many more appear online. To date, the network has received hundreds of thousands of submissions from around the world. Journalists can also use social networks, the online communities outlined in Chapter 9, as a tool for crowdsourcing.

The internet is a very useful tool for news-gathering and reporting, but there are still some records and public information that are not available online. Reporters may still have to search through old, dusty files, but can give them new life by posting the resulting stories on the web. The internet also provides a way for journalists to connect and interact with their audience in ways that were next to impossible before its existence. Writing on the web is about much more than writing and requires not only the reporter, but the audience as well, to contribute to the news-gathering process.

BLOGGING

CHAPTER THREE

A *blog*, short for "web log," is a type of website that displays entries or "posts" in reverse chronological order with the most recent post displayed on the top of the site. A blog is like an online journal that can contain any combination of text, photos, videos, graphics, and links to other websites and can be written by one or more people. The act of creating or updating blog posts is called *blogging* and a person who writes or produces content for a blog is a *blogger*. As of this writing, there are more than 100 million blogs created by internet users around the world that cover an infinite number of topics. Most blogs are updated frequently, sometimes several times a day, once a week, or even once a month. The frequency of posts is completely dependent on the blogger's schedule.

There are many different types of blogs, both personal and professional, which can be used to share news and current events or to share an opinion. Many news media use blogs to share local, national, or international news using the blog format as a means of distribution. These news blogs can be written by professional journalists or anyone with a computer and a passion for sharing news. Some bloggers use the format to share their expertise on specific topics with a global audience. Others use blogs to share personal experiences or their opinion on selected subjects in a format similar to a newspaper column. For years, professional journalists were the only people who could share the news or their opinions with millions of people at once because they had access to broadcast stations and print publications with a built-in audience. Blogs have leveled the playing field so that anyone who wants to write or share their thoughts with the world can do so using the internet as a platform.

For journalists, blogs are a way to interact directly with their audience and communities. Blogs differ from traditional media in that instead of the blogger writing with no expectation of feedback, the audience can directly respond to and comment on posts. Like online news articles, blog posts usually have a space at the end of each post that allows anyone to comment on or discuss the content. Blog posts are often written in a much more conversational style compared to writing for traditional print publications. Posts are also edited less than a traditional news article, often just for spelling, grammar, and fact-checking. This unfiltered approach to writing helps the blogger establish their own distinct voice and creates a more open dialog between the blogger and the audience. Many millions of blogs populate the web so it is important that each blog offer a unique perspective or original content that will help it stand out from an already crowded online marketplace.

Getting started

The first step to creating a blog is deciding on a topic. There are many bloggers that write or report on a range of subjects within a single blog, including general current events or whatever subject the blogger chooses to write about that day. The most successful blogs, however, have a specific focus such as technology, sports, the arts, etc., or cater to a specific audience. Creating a focused topic for your blog helps attract a dedicated audience who is also interested in the same subject. For many journalists, selecting a blog topic is easy: they simply blog about their beat. Sports journalists, for example, blog about their favorite teams, education reporters can focus on local schools, and business reporters blog about the local or national economy. Sometimes, a journalist's beat is a broad topic that covers many other narrower topics or issues. There are often thousands of blogs written about a particular subject, so many blogging journalists cater to a very specific audience within their beat. *The Los Angeles Times*, for example, hosts the blog Funland (*www.latimes. com/travel/deals*), dedicated exclusively to the area's many amusement parks. *The Toronto Star*'s Sound Mind blog (*thestar.blogs.com/soundmind*) covers the city's classical music scene and several bloggers at *The (UK) Guardian* contribute to the site's Mortarboard blog (*www.guardian.co.uk/education/mortarboard*), which covers grade school and university education.

Bloggers can also blog about something that is not specifically related to their beat, but that they are particularly passionate or knowledgeable about. Business reporting, for example, spans a range of subjects. If you are a business reporter and also love shopping, you could create a blog for other business-savvy fashionistas — a topic that falls under your beat, but caters to a particular part of your audience.

With the millions of blogs that already exist on the web, it is difficult to find a topic that isn't already covered. If you choose a topic for which one or several other blogs already exist, do not be discouraged. By introducing a new view or unique approach to an existing topic you can establish yourself as an authority on the subject along existing blogs. There may be several other blogs that cover the same topic, but online readers appreciate multiple points of view and often read several blogs dedicated to the same subject.

People usually read blogs because the blogger shares their interests, so whatever topic you select, it must be something you are passionate about. If you aren't interested or invested in the subject of your blog, your readers won't be either. The topic of your blog should also be something you will not quickly tire of or run out of ideas for. Blogs require a substantial commitment to create and maintain, but if the subject is something you enjoy or are happy to discuss, the commitment will feel less like a burden and more like an enjoyable hobby. No matter the topic, blogging is about establishing authority in your area of expertise. Online readers look to blogs as credible sources of information so you must not only be passionate about the topic, but also able to speak fluently and with authority on the subject. This also means presenting information that is both factual and fact-checked and free from indications of amateur writing such as misspelling, poor grammar, and incoherent thought. Bloggers, especially independent bloggers not backed by an established news organization, must work especially hard to establish credibility with their audience.

After you select a topic, you'll need to create a name for your blog. A blog name should be short and catchy and something the reader can easily remember. Great blog names include *USA Today*'s pop culture blog Pop Candy (*blogs.usatoday.com/popcandy*) or *Time Magazine*'s The Curious Capitalist (*curiouscapitalist.blogs.time.com*), which focuses on the economy. Even if you come up with a great blog name, you'll also need to make sure it hasn't already been taken. Duplicating an existing name makes it less likely that readers will find your blog in a search engine. Before settling on a name for your blog, enter it into a search engine like Google or Yahoo! Search and check the results to see if the name is already being used. If the name you selected appears in the search results, create a list of possible names for your blog, ranked in order from favorite to least favorite. Enter each name into the search engine and eliminate any names that have already been taken. This will reduce the chance that you will duplicate an existing blog name and ensure that the name you select is unique.

For a list of popular news blogs
go to **djhandbook.net/newsblogs**

Blog platforms

To create a blog, you'll need to select a blogging platform — the tool used to create your blog posts and publish them on the web. Many media companies have their own in-house blogging platforms or use publicly available blogging tools. This means newsroom staff do not have to worry about selecting a blog platform or setting up their own blog. If you don't have access to your newsroom's blogging tool or are blogging independently, there are many free and inexpensive blogging platforms to choose from. The most popular blogging tools among journalists and bloggers include WordPress, TypePad, Movable Type, and Blogger.

WordPress, a popular blogging platform among journalists and news organizations, is both a free online blog tool (*www.wordpress.com*) and a downloadable software package that can be installed on an existing site (*www.wordpress.org*). The free version of WordPress lets anyone create their own blog and does not require any real technical skill to set up. Users can sign up for a WordPress blog that is hosted on the WordPress domain (ex: *yourblog. wordpress.com*) and begin blogging right away. Businesses and professional bloggers who want to create blogs that are hosted on their own domain (ex: *www.yoursite.com/blog*) can use WordPress' publicly available blogging software to create a highly customizable blog. The WordPress software is downloaded and installed, usually by someone with web development experience, and offers greater control over the blog's appearance and the features and the functions it includes. WordPress software requires technical knowledge to set up and run, but offers greater flexibility than its free counterpart. Several news organizations use WordPress technology to build and host their own blogs, including *The Wall Street Journal*'s Washington Wire blog (*blogs.wsj.com/washwire*) and several *New York Times* blogs, including Freakonomics (*freakonomics.blogs.nytimes.com*) and Bits Blog (*bits.blogs.nytimes. com*).

TypePad (*www.typepad.com*) is another free blogging tool similar to WordPress that is designed for bloggers with little to no programming experience. There is a small fee to use TypePad, but the platform has features that many free tools don't, including the ability to create photo albums, upload video and audio, and post podcasts. TypePad also has other advanced features like the ability to integrate advertising into a blog. News blogs powered by TypePad include *Entertainment Weekly*'s PopWatch (*popwatch.ew.com*) and the *Wired Magazine* blogs Gadget Lab (*www.wired.com/gadgetlab*) and Wired Science (*www. wired.com/wiredscience*).

Just as WordPress has both a free version and downloadable software, Movable Type (*www.movabletype.org*) is downloadable software and a counterpart to TypePad. Movable Type and TypePad are both distributed by software company Six Apart and are built on the same technology. Movable Type is best for companies, organizations, and professional bloggers who need more advanced options and flexibility. Movable Type allows users to run several blogs or a network of blogs on a single platform and can handle large amounts of traffic. Blogs powered by Movable Type can also be heavily customized by anyone with basic programming skills. Popular news blogs that run on Movable Type include The Huffington Post (*www.huffingtonpost.com*) and Talking Points Memo (*www.talkingpointsmemo.com*).

Blogger (*www.blogger.com*), the free, Google-owned blog platform, is a popular choice among novice and non-professional bloggers. Blogger has a simple and intuitive system that is great for beginners, but does not have many of the advanced features that professional organizations and bloggers require. Like WordPress and TypePad, Blogger users can create and set up their blogs and begin posting within minutes. The site lets users host their blog on the Blogger domain (*yourblog*.blogspot.com) or on their own domain (www.*yourblog*.com).

WordPress (*www.wordpress.org*)

Despite the differences, most blogging platforms have the same basic functions, including the ability to create, format, save, and publish posts. If you have used a word processing program like Microsoft Word, you can easily create your own blog posts. On most blog platforms, the text included in blog posts can be written and formatted and photos and content such as YouTube videos or other online media can be embedded in posts. The process of creating and publishing posts only takes a few minutes, depending on the length of your post.

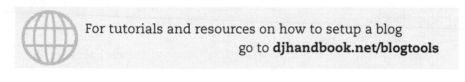

For tutorials and resources on how to setup a blog
go to **djhandbook.net/blogtools**

Beyond the initial setup there is no real technical knowledge required to write for a blog. The blogging platform you choose should be based on your budget and the level of flexibility and customization you require. Many bloggers prefer one platform over the other, but take a tour of each of the tools to see which one is right for you.

Blogroll	# The Newsroom Blog	**About the blog**
	Blogging the News	
	Local group teaches children to sing	
	September 24	
Previous posts		
		Archives
		September
		August
		July
		June
	Tags: children, music | Permalink	May
	12 Comments	April
		March
Recent comments		February
		January
	Movie star visits city	
	September 23	

A typical blog layout

Design

The design of a blog is as — if not more — important than the content itself. Your blog can feature the most compelling and well-written blog posts, but if the site itself is an eyesore or is visually distracting, the visitor may never read them. A new visitor to your blog must be able to quickly tell what the blog is about and identify the posts or content that interests them.

The design of a blog can vary widely and is up to the individual blogger, however, many blogs share common layouts and features. Most blogs consist of three components: the *header*, the *sidebar*, and the *posts* or body of the blog. A blog's header is the online equivalent of a newspaper's masthead. It contains the name or logo of the blog and sometimes a graphic or image that represents what the blog is about. If the blog is a hosted by a news organization, the name of the company should be prominently displayed somewhere in the header so readers can readily associate the blog with the newsroom. Some blog headers also include a *tagline*, a short but descriptive statement of the content or mission of the blog. For example, "Shoppers bite back," the tagline of consumer affairs blog The Consumerist (*www.consumerist.com*), appears below the blog name. A tagline is like a motto or slogan and should spark the reader's interest.

Like printed newspapers, most blogs organize their content into columns. Posts make up the main content of the blog and are usually displayed in the widest column. Posts can include text, photos, images, embedded video, and audio clips and — on some blogs — interactive features such as Flash presentations. Posts themselves consist of several element: the title or headline that describes the post, the body, which contains text or any of the aforementioned media, and the date and time when the post was published, which identifies when the post was written. If a blog has more than one author, the name of the author is usually included at the beginning or end of each post.

Writing post after post with just text will create a block of posts which, save for the headlines, cannot be differentiated from one other without actually reading each entry. A good blog also incorporates some visual element in addition to text, usually photos or other images that illustrate the subject of the post. This visual element can be, for example, a photo of a person or event that is the subject of the post. Adding relevant images to posts gives each one a unique look and helps breaks up long paragraphs of text.

Most blogs feature a space immediately below each post that includes a list of recent comments, similar to those found on online articles and news sites, as well as a way for readers to add their own comments. Other features that sometimes appear below or near blog posts include a short list of related posts the reader may also find interesting and *trackbacks*, brief bits of text that show other sites that have linked to that blog post. Trackbacks usually include a brief snippet of text and a link back to the site or blog that referenced the post. These trackbacks can appear adjacent to comments in a separate block or mixed in with regular comments. Some blog posts also feature a *permalink*, a unique web address that is used as a direct link to the post. Permalinks are used to share a blog post elsewhere on the web including e-mail, instant messages, social networks, or other blogs.

Another common component of a blog is the *sidebar*, a space so named because it appears on one or both sides of the main body of the blog, adjacent to the posts. A sidebar can be customized to include any combination of elements the blogger selects. Common components found in a blog's sidebar include a short biography, a way for users to subscribe to the blog, advertisements, and a *blogroll*. A blogroll is a list of links to blogs that the blogger recommends to his or her readers. The blogroll can include blogs with similar topics or — for news blogs — other blogs from the same newsroom. Bloggers can also include links to other non-blog websites.

Some blog sidebars also feature a list of previously written posts and/or popular posts that the reader may also find interesting. These lists can be generated automatically depending on the blogging platform and are often used to direct readers to other posts or areas of the site. Some blogs also include a short list of recent comments that readers have posted to the blog and are used to prompt further discussion.

Many blogs sort posts by categories or *tags*, descriptive keywords or brief phrases that describe the focus or subject of the post. Tags help categorize the content of a blog and direct readers to posts with similar topics. For example, a blog about pets may have posts dedicated to different animals such as cats, dogs, or birds. By tagging each entry with the name of the animal that is the subject of the post, readers can find all the posts that have been written about birds, all the posts written about cats, and so on. The tags assigned to each entry usually appear at the bottom of the post and a list of tags used on the blog is featured in the sidebar. A blog can accumulate many different tags so some blogs only feature the most commonly used tags in the sidebar.

Most blogs only display the most recent posts — usually about five to ten — on the front page. As newer posts are written, older posts are pushed out of the front page, but are still available in the site's *archives*. A blog's archive categorizes posts by the date they were published, usually by month, but sometimes by week or by day, and generates a list of dates that appears in the sidebar. Archives allow readers to search for posts written on a specific date and, along with tags, help visitors find older posts after they no longer appear on the front page. Readers can also use a blog's *search* function, a feature often integrated into a blog to help readers find specific topics or keywords mentioned on the site. The search function is often a box included at the top of the site or in the sidebar and is similar to a *search engine*, but only searches for content on one particular site or blog.

Blogs often have one or more writers and readers want to know who they are and how to contact them. A short biography for each blogger should be featured somewhere on the site and can include contact information such as e-mail or a phone number as well as a photo of the blogger.

There are many different features that can be built into a blog and bloggers should include whatever components they feel will complement the site. Each component is selected by the blogger or a blog administrator, the person who designs or manages the blog. The administrator controls many of the blog's features and functions and may not be the person doing the actual blogging. If making technical changes to the structure of your blog is outside of your skill set, don't worry. Many blogging platforms such as WordPress, TypePad, and Blogger have thousands of pre-designed templates to choose from and allow the blogger to select the features they want to see on their blog. Templates can take some of the guesswork out of design and allow the blogger to focus on creating content instead of the technical issues of building a blog.

Other types of blogs

In traditional blogging, posts consist mostly of text with other supporting visual elements. There are, however, other forms of blogging in which media that would otherwise be a supporting element make up the bulk of the content of the blog.

For example, on most blogs, photos are included in posts to support the text. On a *photoblog*, a blog that consists mostly of photographs, the photos are the main feature and are supported by a limited amount of text or commentary. Posts on a photoblog can feature a single photo or a group of photos focused on a particular subject or taken at a certain time. Photoblogs can be created and managed by a single photographer to showcase his or her work or can feature the work of a group of photographers, either from a single newsroom or from various photojournalists around the world. Boston.com's The Big Picture (*www.boston.com/bigpicture*), a popular photoblog with collections of recent news photos, is an example of the latter. Each post is dedicated to a single topic and usually includes 20 to 30 photographs from photographers around the world. Like many other photoblogs, the images that appear on The Big Picture are displayed as large as possible on a relatively small computer screen to maximize the impact on the viewer.

While text is usually not a prominent feature of photoblogs, it is important that each image be accompanied by a caption or small paragraph of text that describes the subject of the photo and includes information about where the photo was taken and by whom. This text helps search engines that cannot "see" the content of the image index the blog and direct people searching for specific keywords to the site. Photoblogs can also include headlines, datelines, and other features found on a regular blog.

 For examples of popular photoblogs, as well as how to create one go to **djhandbook.net/photoblogs**

The Newsroom Photoblog

Tourists at the beach during the summer
February 10, 12:31 p.m.

12 Comments

A typical photoblog layout

A *videoblog* or *vlog* is an ongoing series of videos either embedded in individual blog posts or a series of similarly themed video clips that are posted to a website or online video sharing service such as YouTube. Like regular blogs, a *videoblog* can cover a range of topics and are presented in many different formats.

Videoblogs can be an unscripted chat with the viewing audience where, instead of writing, the vlogger talks directly to the camera and shares opinions or thoughts on a predetermined topic such as a current event or news story. Vlog posts can also include on-camera interviews where guests join the vlogger for a chat about a given subject. Another type of video blog is the "how-to" vlog that instructs the viewer on how to do or create something. This can be anything from a step-by-step guide on how to fix a leaky faucet to instructions on how to ride a bike. For example, CHOW (*www.chow.com*), a popular site for recipes and cooking tips, regularly posts food-related video guides of everything from how to cook fried chicken to how to clean a coffee maker. Journalists can also use videoblogs to offer a behind the scenes look at their stories or as an informal discussion with viewers.

A typical videoblog layout

The Star-Ledger, for example, hosts Ledger Live (*www.nj.com/ledgerlive*), a videoblog that features live video from the field, commentary on recent news events, and dispatches from the newsroom.

A good videoblog should be lively, engaging, and most of all relatively brief. Many vlog posts are improvised as they are recorded, meaning vloggers can post long and unrestricted on-camera discussions. To avoid digression, decide ahead of time what you want to discuss in your vlog post and make a list of the key points you want to discuss. Like a photoblog, a videoblog should also include text summary adjacent to the video that describes what the viewer should expect to see.

 For examples of popular videoblogs, as well as how to create one go to **djhandbook.net/videoblogs**

Instead of paragraphs of text, *linkblogs* consist mostly of links to articles or news stories from around the web, sometimes accompanied by a brief summary or commentary on the content of the link. The links are selected by a blogger or editor who selects interesting online content that he or she thinks others will want to read. Linkblogs are different from regular blogs in that the blogger usually relies on the content others create to populate their own blog. Popular linkblogs include Drudge Report (*www.drudgereport.com*) founded by noted blogger Matt Drudge and Kottke.org (*www.kottke.org*), curated and edited by blogger Jason Kottke. Linkblogs can be dedicated to a specific subject like Drudge Report, which features links to political news, or be a collection of interesting links that have no relation to each other like those featured on Kottke.org. Both blogs include links to a variety of sources and feature online stories, articles, or other content the author finds compelling. A large percentage of the time required to run a linkblog is dedicated to searching the web for great content to link to. If the blogger consistently directs readers to interesting online content, they will often return to the site for more.

Journalists can use linkblogs to share stories or articles they are reading or source material they are including in future stories. For example, *The New York Times*' "Diner's Journal" blog (*http://nyti.ms/ffdlhW*) regularly features "What We're Reading," a collection of shared links by the reporters and editors of the newsroom's dining section.

The Newsroom Linkblog

Linking to the News

October 20

Daily Times: Politician in hot water

The Journal: Crime rate down

Online News: New trees planted in park

---

14 Comments

October 19

A typical linkblog layout

Linkblogs can be created by hand where the blogger copy and pastes links into a post or can be created automatically using social bookmarking tools like Diigo (*www.diigo.com*) or Publish2 (*www.publish2.com*). Both sites allow users to save links and add optional comments which can then be automatically posted to a blog.

 For examples of popular linkblogs, as well as how to create one go to **djhandbook.net/linkblogs**

A *liveblog* is a blog or a single post on a blog that contains real-time updates that are posted during and in response to a particular event such as a court proceeding, sports event, award show, political speech or natural disaster. On a liveblog, the blogger posts brief updates that contain observations or opinions that give readers a feel for the atmosphere or response to an event. A regular blog post may be written in reaction to an event that happened days or weeks or before, but a liveblog often provides up-to-the-minute coverage that online readers can follow as the event is happening. Staff reporters for *Entertainment Weekly* (*www.ew.com*), for example, often liveblog awards shows like the Academy Awards or the Grammys which have a loyal following, but which most readers cannot physically attend. These liveblogs offer an inside view or a unique and humorous perspective on a particular event and are popular among the site's readers.

The Newsroom Blog

Blogging the News

Liveblog of the mayor's speech
January 30

8:30 AM:

8:46 AM:

9:03 AM:

9:14 AM:

47 Comments

A typical liveblog layout

For a liveblog, each short post is time-stamped and posted above the previous one in reverse chronological order. This means a reader checking for updates will see the most recent update at the top of the post. Whether the blog is presented in chronological or reverse chronological order depends on the style of the individual news organization and how many live visitors the site is expecting. Some liveblogs may have a low number of people following along as it is written, but because of the longevity of the web, many internet users read liveblogs long after the event has happened as a recap of what happened. If a large number of readers follow the liveblog as it is updated, it is best to post the most recent updates at the top, so they can be seen quickly without requiring the reader to scroll to the bottom of the page.

The key to a successful liveblog is to let readers know well ahead of time that the event will be covered and remind them again just before the event begins. There are several online tools that make liveblogging easier. CoveritLive (*www.coveritlive.com*) provides an instant message-like approach to liveblogging and allows the blogger to post photos and video and audio clips, in addition to text. Livebloggers can also send updates from a cell phone using the microblogging tool Twitter (*www.twitter.com*).

 For examples of popular liveblogs, as well as how to create one go to **djhandbook.net/liveblogs**

RSS

Many online readers don't read blog posts on the actual site, but through an RSS feed. RSS, short for "Really Simple Syndication," is a system for distributing news and other regularly updated online content. An RSS feed allows anyone to "subscribe" to a blog or website and be automatically notified when new posts, articles, or stories have been posted on a site. Using an RSS *reader*, an online tool or downloadable software for organizing RSS feeds, anyone can read the content of multiple blogs or sites without visiting each site individually. RSS allows online readers to create news feeds tailored to their interests by adding their favorite sites to their RSS reader. The reader scans the feeds the user selects for any updates and aggregates them in a single destination. RSS allows readers to receive news updates from a variety of sites and varying points of view.

Popular RSS readers include Google Reader (*reader.google.com*) and Bloglines (*www.bloglines.com*) which can retrieve content from any RSS-enabled site with regularly updated content, not just blogs. RSS feeds can also be set to deliver directly to an e-mail address, but depending on the number of sites you subscribe to, this method can quickly become overwhelming. In technical terms, RSS is an XML feed that monitors a site for new content, but there is no technical knowledge required to use RSS.

The majority of news sites and blogs offer RSS feeds as a service to readers. A blog or site can offer a single RSS feed that delivers all the site's content or offer multiple feeds dedicated to specific areas of the site. *The New York Times* (*www.nytimes.com/rss*), for example, offers RSS feeds for each section of its site and for each of its blogs. *The Times'* "World" section has its own catchall RSS feed, but also has individual RSS feeds dedicated to Africa, the Americas, Asia Pacific, Europe, and the Middle East. Because of the large number of sections on its site, the Times has roughly 100 different feeds to which millions of online readers collectively subscribe. Some news sites also offer custom RSS feeds that let the reader select their own topic or set of topics and create an RSS feed tailored to their reading habits or needs.

Website administrators can control the amount of content that appears in the site's RSS feed. Feeds can contain full posts or articles or feature just a brief paragraph or summary or just headlines with links to the full story. Many news sites offer abbreviated feeds that require the reader to visit the website to view the rest of the content.

If you provide an RSS feed for your blog or site, you must let your readers know that it exists and make it easy for them to subscribe. Most sites do this by placing an RSS icon somewhere on the page, usually near the top of the site, with a link to the page where the reader can subscribe. The RSS icon it its original form looks like a rounded orange square with three white wavelines, but can take various, more creative forms. Some sites also feature a link that says "Click here to subscribe" that

An RSS icon

directs the visitor to a page where they can subscribe to one or more RSS feeds. Many online readers now expect every website with regularly updated content to feature an RSS feed. Every blog or website should have at least one feed available for potential subscribers.

RSS is also a valuable tool for journalists. Reporters can monitor news from a range of online sources in one place, which makes it easier to keep up with breaking news and relevant updates. Using RSS for news-gathering is as easy as finding blogs or sites that cover news or topics relevant your beat and adding to them to an RSS reader. RSS readers also allow users to tag or filter each feed by subject, further reducing the time necessary to keep track of online content.

For tutorials on how to create and use RSS feeds, as well a guide to recommended feeds for journalists go to **djhandbook.net/rss**

Creating a successful blog

There are many blogs on the internet, but the most successful are those that produce content that is timely, useful, and engaging. Great bloggers post unique content or commentary that readers can't find anywhere else on the web. The internet is populated with many millions of blogs so to stand out from the crowd it is necessary to offer readers a fresh perspective that defines your blog. In traditional print journalism, news stories from a single publication are written in an editorial voice that varies only slightly from reporter to reporter. The opposite is true for bloggers, even those writing under the watch of a traditional media company. Individual journalists should develop their own style of blogging and express themselves by infusing their writing with vivid language that reflects their personality. Online readers are attracted to unique voices and tend to shy away from dry or formulaic writing.

Remember that blogging is not just a one-way conversation. The medium is a way to generate discussion around a particular topic or issue. Great blogs build online communities and encourage user interaction by asking questions and encouraging feedback from readers. Bloggers can share their opinion, but the best blogs also invite readers to share their opinions or comments as well. This open dialog is one of hallmarks of digital journalism along with interactivity and collaboration. Like regular online news stories, blog posts can attract comments, both good and bad. However, a few bad comments should not dissuade you from interacting and responding to readers. Even if negative comments become overwhelming, do not eliminate or disable your blog's comment feature. A blog with no comment section is just a one-sided conversation, and violates the previously mentioned principles of the web.

Bloggers can use the comment section, along with other forms of communication such as an e-mail address or telephone number, as a way to solicit suggestions on how to improve a blog and its content. Rather than guess at the topics or posts that readers like or prefer, bloggers can also use *analytics* to track which posts are most popular and how visitors are finding the blog and its individual posts. Using analytics to study the behavior of readers can create a more effective blog that more accurately focuses on the needs or desires of its audience. Analytics can also have a downside. It is easy to fall in the trap of writing only what you think readers will want to read. Relying too heavily on analytics can cause a blogger to lose focus or worse — feel compelled to write posts that aren't interesting to the author. Writing posts about issues or topics that fascinate or appeal to you means you will write more passionately about the subject, which will in turn attract like-minded readers.

Sometimes bloggers write posts that are intentionally controversial or take an unpopular stand to generate traffic or links back to their blog. This is referred to as *linkbait* because it can increase the number of links to or mentions of the blog, but it can also damage a blog's credibility. For example, in 2009, *Wired Magazine* published the online article "Twitter, Flickr, Facebook Make Blogs Look So 2004" in which the author inferred that blogs with smaller audiences were obsolete and no longer necessary because they couldn't compete with larger blogs like The Huffington Post (*www.huffingtonpost.com*). The story was heavily circulated around the web and generated a negative response both to the article and to the magazine. Many bloggers wrote responses condemning the article while others chastised *Wired* for running what they saw as an intentionally inflammatory editorial.

Bloggers may intentionally or unintentionally write posts that spark controversy because the web is, after all, a platform for anyone to express and share their opinion. However, a blog isn't the place for professional journalists to vent their frustrations or to make wild assertions and libelous statements. Doing so is a surefire way to lose your credibility and possibly your job. Avoid tirades and attacking others, as you still represent your newsroom and yourself. Some journalists go outside of the constrictions of the newsroom and create independent blogs that may or not reflect their beat or employer. These blogs can be anything from an account of their personal life and family to a discussion of their interests or hobbies. It is important to remember that while an independent blog may not be associated with the newsroom and does not carry the name of the news organization, if it features the reporter's name it can possibly be traced back to the reporter's employer. Inappropriate online behavior or controversial statements can be seen as a reflection of newsroom, whether you intend them to or not. Therefore, it is best to regard an independent blog and its content as an extension of the newsroom, even though there may be no formal connection between the two.

Like any form of print journalism, blogs should be free from spelling and grammatical errors, which can hurt the blogger's credibility. Poor writing is distracting and though everything may be factual and true, readers will see the writing as amateur. In some newsrooms, blog posts are read by an editor or supervisor before they are posted to the web to check for accuracy and mistakes. In many cases, however, posts are not reviewed before they are published on the web. It is therefore necessary that each blog post be reread from beginning to end before it is posted. Each post should be checked for spelling mistakes, grammar, cohesive thought, correct links, and other potential errors.

Treat each post like it is the first and last the reader will ever see, because often it is. Older posts are indexed by search engines like Google and may be read months or years after they were first written. Readers who are searching for keywords that match the content featured on the blog may find your posts, which can serve as a gateway to the rest of the blog's content.

A trait many successful bloggers share is that they follow other blogs with similar topics to stay abreast of what others are discussing on the web. Reading material outside of your own blog can help inform your posts and is similar to a news reporter checking with sources before writing a story. Linking to helpful or interesting posts found on other blogs is a great service to readers who appreciate diverse opinions and further resources on a particular subject. If you refer to information found on another blog, do not copy or steal whole posts or present another blogger's reporting as your own. This is plagiarism and violates the ethics of journalism. Instead, include a few sentences or paragraphs in your post and link back to the original article as a form of attribution.

Though many news media are now responsible for a large percentage of blogs, not long ago journalists actively distanced themselves from bloggers, who they saw as less credible than a credentialed reporter in a professional newsroom. Journalists saw bloggers as amateurs with no editorial oversight, writing whatever they wished without restraint. While this may still be true for some bloggers, a growing percentage of blogs not affiliated with a major news organization have professional editorial processes in place and share the same standards as traditional journalists. Many independent bloggers are as influential and highly regarded as their mainstream media counterparts, often filling the void of news not reported by traditional media. Drudge Report, for example, rose to fame after the site broke news of U.S. President Bill Clinton's affair with intern Monica Lewinsky before it was reported by a mainstream news organization. The blog is now visited by millions of users a month is responsible for a significant portion of the traffic directed to mainstream news sites. A single link from Drudge Report can direct hundreds of thousands of visitors to a news site within hours after it is posted.

Blogs — even those written as a hobby — require a substantial commitment to update and maintain. Some bloggers have a set schedule of when they actually write each blog post, while others write posts whenever inspiration strikes. Like physical exercise, it's easy to get stressed out from blogging if you do it too much. If blogging becomes a burden, try lightening your writing schedule. For example, if you write two to three posts a day, try writing one really good post each day. If your blog is updated once daily, consider writing just a few posts a week. Writing a few good entries is better than writing a lot of bad ones. Blog posts don't have to be written all at once either. Many blogging platforms allow bloggers to write and save their posts for later or publish them at a future date or time.

To help make the blogging process easier, write down ideas when you think of them and flesh them out later when you have time. Ideas for blog posts can come at any moment, so it is best to write them down when inspiration strikes rather than write a post when you have nothing to say. You don't have to write the full post, but it does help to have a running list of possible posts for days when you are struggling to come up with ideas. After you blog for a while, you will undoubtedly find a schedule that works best for you. If you truly don't feel like blogging one day, don't. The blog will still be there the next day, so stick with it even it means taking a break. Whatever you do, don't disappear and leave readers wondering what happened. If you sense that blogging is not for you, create a post that explains why you have chosen to discontinue the blog.

Blogging is undoubtedly a tough job and takes persistence and dedication to develop a significant following. Many novice bloggers often become frustrated when they don't attract large numbers of visitors or comments within the first few months of blogging. Before you begin blogging or even if you've already started, consider that it may take some time before your blog receives a substantial audience. Even the most popular blogs didn't become popular overnight — some took months or even years before they gained a loyal audience of readers. A blog may not become popular immediately, but over time can attract a significant following. As news of your blog and its content spreads, the number of visitors will inevitably grow.

PHOTOGRAPHY

📷

CHAPTER FOUR

Photojournalism — the art of telling stories with photographs — is used to document the people and places in the news in a way text alone cannot. A single photo can capture emotion and communicate a story without words. Photos have long have had a place in journalism, but with the rise of online technology, traditional news photos are getting a digital makeover. There are many ways photos are posted and presented online. They can appear alone with descriptive captions, be grouped together in photo stories, or arranged in a *slideshow,* a collection of similarly themed photos displayed in sequence, one after the other. Many online news sites feature photo slideshows that together tell a story or showcase the work of one or more photographers. For example, MSNBC's "Week in Pictures" (*www.msnbc.msn.com/id/3842331*) uses photo slideshows to display captivating news photos shot by photographers around the world. News photos can also be published in *photoblogs* such as *The Wall Street Journal*'s "Photo Journal" (*blogs.wsj.com/photojournal*), in which news photos from each week are featured in individual blog posts. There are a variety of technologies used to display photos online, but at the center of each format are compelling news photographs that tell stories visually.

Photojournalism was once the sole domain of professional news photographers who were dedicated exclusively to the craft. Now, traditional print and broadcast reporters are also required to take photos, in addition to writing and reporting stories. Reporters aren't the only ones required to multitask: veteran photojournalists are also equipped with additional multimedia tools such as video cameras or audio recorders to capture stories in other media besides photography. Years ago, being a photojournalist meant lugging around a heavy camera and tons of equipment, but as digital cameras have become smaller and cheaper there is less of a barrier to professional photography. The increased popularity of inexpensive cameras and camera phones means professional journalists aren't the only ones snapping photos of news events as they happen. There is, however, a level of training and conscious attention to composition that separates photojournalism from a simple snap of the camera. By learning how to properly operate a camera and how to shoot a well-composed photograph, even non-visual journalists can master the basics of photojournalism.

Choosing a camera

The first step to shooting photos is deciding which type of camera to use. There are many different models to choose from with various capabilities, some of which are made for novice photographers and others that are equipped with scores of advanced features. Photo cameras used by professional journalists have one thing in common: they capture digital images. Digital cameras make the process of shooting, selecting, and posting photos faster than what is possible with traditional film cameras.

Digital cameras can be categorized into three groups: point-and-shoot, professional, and *prosumer*, a camera that is both easy to use and includes professional features. A point-and-shoot camera has few or no manual controls and allows the photographer to simply point the camera at a subject and press a button to take a photo. Consumer-level point-and-shoot cameras are geared toward novice photographers and have fewer features than a professional camera. You don't have to know how a camera works to operate a point-and-shoot, making it a great choice for beginning photographers. Some more advanced point-and-shoot cameras also have manual controls and features to give the photographer greater control over the images. Point-and-shoot cameras are usually relatively small and can fit comfortably in a pants or shirt pocket.

The number of photos a digital camera can store depends on the *resolution* of the photographs, or the level of detail in each digital image. Digital photos are made of tiny dots called *pixels*, a series of points that together make up an image. High-resolution photographs have more pixels which means they are much more detailed than a photo with fewer pixels. Photographs that appear in print require more detail and are usually shot in a higher resolution. Low-resolution photographs are less detailed and work well for the web. News photos should ideally be shot at the highest resolution possible — even if the photos will appear solely on the web — so they can be used in several media. Photo editors can decrease the size of a high-resolution photo into a lower-resolution image, but doing the reverse makes photos look blurry and distorted.

Many point-and-shoot cameras have the same basic features, including automatic flash and focus, the ability to zoom, and a built-in LCD screen. LCD, short for liquid crystal display, is a flat screen featured on many digital cameras that is used to compose and view photos. LCD screens allow photographers to instantly preview what the photograph will look like, see photos after they are taken, and delete them if necessary. The LCD screen is also used to access the digital camera's menu system where users can change settings and access features. Most point-and-shoot cameras are equipped with LCD screens, but are also equipped with a *viewfinder*, a small, usually rectangular opening in a camera, used to compose the image without electronic assistance.

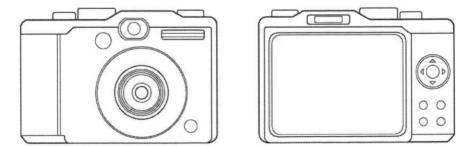

A typical point-and-shoot camera

Most point-and-shoot digital cameras are equipped with *optical zoom*, a feature that allows the photographer to obtain a closer or further image of a subject without physically moving the camera. When the camera zooms in, the camera electronically adjusts the focus to get a closer image. When the camera is zoomed out, the camera widens the focus to capture more of the scene. The zoom button is usually a rocker or set of buttons on top of the camera, sometimes marked "T" for toward and "W" for withdraw. Some digital cameras are also equipped with *digital zoom*, an electronic feature that appears to zoom in even closer to the subject than traditional optical zoom. Digital zoom doesn't actually zoom further — instead it crops the edges of the digital image to make it appear as if it is closer to the subject. Cropping a photo this way can cause *pixelation*, or blurry or reduced-quality photographs. For this reason, digital zoom should not be used by professional photographers.

The photo on the right is zoomed in and closer to the subject

Point-and-shoot cameras are usually equipped with *flash*, also called a *strobe*, which creates a short burst of light that illuminates the subject being photographed. A built-in flash is generally positioned above or near the camera's *lens*, the circular feature on the front of the camera used to capture the photograph. The amount of light received by the camera's sensor is called the *exposure*. If there is too much light, the photo is *overexposed* and the image will be washed out or bright splotches of light will appear in the photo. If there is not enough light, the photograph is *underexposed* and the photograph will appear too dark. Underexposed photos taken with a digital camera can also contain "noise" or appear grainy. This problem occurs when the camera's sensor does not have enough information to render the image correctly. To avoid these potential problems, almost all point-and-shoot cameras have automatic flash mode, a setting that instinctively triggers the flash when the camera senses there isn't enough light to capture the subject.

The flash from a basic point-and-shoot camera can cast harsh, unnatural shadows on the subject. Many cameras include several different flash modes that, depending on the available light, alter the strength of flash. These settings include red-eye reduction mode, which minimizes the red circles that appear in the eyes of the subject, a common problem found in photographs taken with a flash. Instead of firing a single burst of light, a camera set to red-eye reduction mode first flashes lower bursts of light, then the main flash. The initial bursts of light cause the iris of the eye to contract, meaning less light fills the eye and reduces the chance that the subject's eyes will appear red in a photograph.

Automatic flash and red-eye reduction mode are examples of *presets*, predetermined settings created by the camera's manufacturer to optimize photos depending on the scene being captured. Many cameras have preset controls for common subjects or settings such as landscapes, night photos, and portraits. Some digital cameras, including basic point-and-shoot cameras, are equipped with *image stabilization*, a feature that digitally compensates for shaking caused by handheld photography and makes photos appear less blurry. Some cameras are also equipped with *autofocus*, a feature that automatically analyzes the distance from the camera to the selected subject and electronically adjusts the focus accordingly.

Most basic point-and-shoot-cameras use a USB connection to transfer images from the camera to a computer. USB, short for Universal Serial Bus, is a system for connecting a computer to other electronic equipment and is standard on modern computers. To transfer images using a USB connection, one end of a USB cable is connected to the computer and the other end to the camera. A folder that contains the digital images can then be accessed from the computer. For a detailed explanation of this process, consult the manual included with your digital camera.

Despite the obvious benefits of point-and-shoot cameras, there are some downsides which make them less useful for professional news photographers. The most common problem is that some point-and-shoot cameras can take a full second or more after the *shutter* button — the button that tells the camera

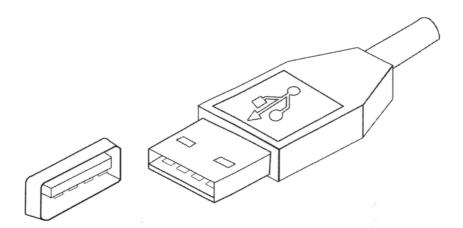

A USB connection and plug

to snap a picture — is pressed before the photo is actually taken. This delay is called *shutter lag* because before the camera captures the image, the camera focuses and calculates the exposure before it actually records the photo. This delay can cause the photographer to miss a moment, which is not acceptable in news photography. Point-and-shoot cameras also do not perform well in low light. Higher-end cameras have a built-in or an attachable strobe light that is often more powerful than the camera's built-in flash and allows greater control over the light emitted by the camera. Photographers can also use a *light kit*, a set of professional lamps and accessories used to control the light in a scene. Light kits are not as useful when shooting photos in the field or if the subject is moving because they are bulky and require time to set up.

For professional results, news photographers should use a *single-lens reflex* or SLR camera. A digital SLR camera is called a *DSLR*. An SLR camera differs from a point-and-shoot in that the image is viewed through the same lens that takes the photo. SLRs use a mirror that lets the photographer look through the viewfinder to see an accurate representation of the image they are about to capture. When the photographer presses the shutter button, the mirror flips up, allowing the camera's sensor to record the image. Some DSLRs are also equipped with LCD screens, which gives the photographer the option to use one or both methods to view and frame photographs.

SLR cameras are often larger and more rugged than most point-and-shoot cameras and capture higher quality images. SLR cameras also have almost no shutter lag, which makes getting that split-second shot a lot easier and faster. SLRs also perform better under low light than point-and-shoots because of their ability to capture higher resolution photos. SLRs are often pricier than basic point-and-shoot cameras and are equipped with advanced features that allow the photographer to control the camera's functions such as focus and exposure. Some SLR cameras also have interchangeable lenses, which allows the photographer to select the lens that is perfect for the scene.

A typical digital SLR camera

Instead of film, professional digital cameras record and store photos on an internal hard drive or on memory cards. Memory cards are removable storage devices, usually about the size of a large postage stamp, that can hold varying amounts of photos or other digital media depending on the capacity of the card. Some computers are equipped with slots for inserting and reading memory cards, but more often photographers use a *memory card reader*, an external drive that is attached to the computer. A card reader allows the photographer to remove the memory card from the camera and insert it into the card reader which is connected to the computer. Once the card is inserted in the reader, a folder appears on the computer that contains the digital images.

Some SLR cameras are capable of shooting in automatic mode just like a point-and-shoot camera and some point-and-shoot cameras come with professional features and manual controls. These types of cameras are sometimes called *prosumer* cameras. "Prosumer" is a contraction of "professional" and "consumer" and signifies that a camera that combines the ease of a point-and-shoot camera with the features of a professional SLR camera. Prosumer cameras are popular in many newsrooms because they bridge the gap between amateur

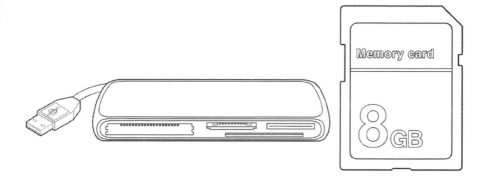

A memory card reader (left) and memory card (enlarged to show detail)

photographers and professional photography.

The type of camera you select should be based on your experience and your budget. While an SLR camera can take high-quality photos, it won't instantly transform an inexperienced photographer into an expert. If you are a novice photographer or are experimenting with photography, consider starting with a point-and-shoot camera. Become familiar with the camera's settings and how it functions. Once you master a basic camera, you'll be ready to upgrade to a camera with more advance settings and controls.

For a guide to photo cameras commonly used by journalists
go to **djhandbook.net/photocameras**

Composing a photo

The gap between amateur and professional photography isn't that wide or difficult to master. The key to taking great photos is learning a few simple guidelines that will produce more aesthetically pleasing and professional-looking photographs. Photojournalists, even more so than regular photographers, aim to tell a story or create a narrative in each photo. A news photo is like a visual story that needs no translation and should be both an introduction to the subject and capture the emotion of the scene. Photojournalism at its core is about documenting news subjects or reactions to an event so the news audience can indirectly experience the drama or emotion of the scene. Emotion can be anything from a grieving mother reacting to the loss of a child to an athlete celebrating a victory after a game.

The first step to capturing a news photo is to find a subject that will serve as the focus of the photo. The subject of many news photographs is often a person, not an object, because readers are attracted to and can connect with faces. Magazines, for example, feature people on their covers to draw the attention of a casual passerby who can connect with the eyes of the person on the cover. This in turn encourages him or her to pick up and read the publication. Including only a person or their face in a photo, however, doesn't tell much of a story. A *headshot* — a close-up photo of just the subject's head and shoulders — shows what someone looks like, but doesn't say much about who the person is or why they were photographed. A photo that tells a story also includes some of the subject's environment in the frame to provide more information about who they are. For example, a photo of a teacher that only includes the person and nothing else could be a photo of anyone. By including a teacher's natural environment such as a school or a classroom in the background of the photo, the viewer understands that the person is a teacher. The same is true for breaking news photography. Victims of natural disasters, for example, are often photographed near the destruction to communicate the gravity of the scene.

The photo on the right shows more of the subject's environment

Some of the best news photos are shot in the peak moment of action, such as a car swerving around a corner or a diver leaping into water. Even if the subject of a photo is an inanimate object, including people in the image gives the photo a sense of perspective and energy. For example, a photo of a building with no one in it can come across as empty and cold. Including people in the photograph, even if they are not the subject of the photo, gives the image a sense of energy and life.

Once you decide what to photograph, you will next need to consider how to compose the photo to communicate the story or narrative you are trying to capture. Consciously composing a photograph instead of just picking up the camera and shooting is what separates professional photographers from amateurs.

One of the basic rules of photo composition is the *rule of thirds* which dictates that when composing a photo, the photographer should mentally divide the image into thirds, both vertically and horizontally, similar to a tic-tac-toe board. Instead of placing your subject in the exact center of the frame — something many novice photographers tend to do — move the subject slightly off-center at one of the four intersecting points on the imaginary grid. This alignment creates a more interesting and dynamic photo.

The above photos are composed according to the rule of thirds

When composing an image, photographers should frame the photo so there are no distracting elements in the background of the photograph. For example, trees and telephone poles positioned behind the subject can appear as if they are growing out of the subject's head or body. Bright lights and colors that appear behind the subject can also distract from the focus of the photo. News photos can include the subject's environment, but the background should be simple enough so the subject is the focus of the image. Also, avoid framing the photograph so that the image ends at one of the body's natural cutoff lines such as the neck, elbows, waist, knees, or ankles. Framing the photo this way can make the subject look like an amputee. Instead, frame the photo so it ends at the subject's chest or the middle of the thigh, which sends a visual cue to the viewer that the body extends beyond the frame of the photograph.

The photo on the left is cropped at the joints; the one on the right is framed at natural cutoff lines

Photographers should also be aware of the angle of the *horizon*, the imaginary line where the land meets the sky. In most cases, the horizon line should be straight and level. An uneven horizon is caused by tilting the camera, which can make the subject appear as if it is leaning at an odd angle. This can be easily corrected by holding the camera so it is level with the ground.

The horizon in the photo on the left is askew; the horizon in the photo on right is level

Taking photos outdoors can present its own issues, especially on a bright, sunny day. Photographers should avoid placing the subject between the camera and the sun, especially when shooting with a basic digital camera. Instead of focusing on the subject, the camera captures the light shining behind it and creates *backlighting*, a halo effect that makes the subject appear dark and obscured. When shooting people, backlighting darkens the subject's face, making them look shadowy or mysterious. Instead, position the camera so the sun is behind you and shining on the subject, creating enough light to properly capture the scene.

The face of the woman in the photo is obscured because the sun is shining behind her

Shooting photos when clouds appear overhead can also diffuse the harsh light caused by direct sunlight. If this is not an option, use the camera's flash to fill in the light and illuminate the subject. Some photographers intentionally shoot during the "golden hour," the hour after sunrise and before sunset when there is a golden hue in the sky that diffuses the sunlight and gives photos a warm color. The light emitted during the golden hour creates a richer and more dynamic photograph.

There are many rules and guidelines to photography, but much of the craft is built on instinct. After you've learned the basics of what makes a great photograph, composing interesting images becomes second nature. Once you know the rules, you can then break them and develop your own style of photography. The best way to improve your photos is by experience, so take your camera everywhere — to parties, weddings or wherever there is an opportunity to hone your skills. After snapping a sufficient number of photos, take a moment and look at your images closely. Think about what makes them good or bad, how the rules of photography came into play, and, most importantly, how the photographs capture the subject and communicate a story.

 For more photography guidelines and examples
go to **djhandbook.net/composition**

Shooting in the field

Before you head out to shoot photos and document a story, you should first collect and prepare your gear, including the camera, memory cards, and extra batteries. Some news photographers carry these items in a specially designed camera bag, while others wear vests with several pockets so they can carry equipment, but are still free to move about. Be sure to clean the camera lens before each shoot with a lens cloth and lens-cleaning fluid to reduce possible blurriness or distortion in your photos. These materials are made exclusively for cleaning cameras, unlike paper napkins or clothing which can scratch or damage the camera lens.

When shooting news photography, keep the camera close and ready to fire. Photojournalism requires skill and thought, but is also about timing and luck. You never know when the action will happen so you should be prepared when that once-in-a-lifetime moment happens. While it is important to keep the camera ready, it is also important that you be aware of your surroundings. If you always keep the camera up to your eye, you may miss the action that's taking place behind or to the side of you.

When you begin shooting, experiment by taking the same photo several different ways — get close-ups, stand back, shoot from different angles, hold the camera both horizontally and vertically, and change the camera's perspective. Don't be afraid to get close or invade personal space to record details such as wrinkled hands or the petals of a flower. Photographers must kneel, crouch, lean, or lay flat to capture great photos. Approaching the subject from the front and standing still is usually enough to get a decent photo, but the extra effort creates a more interesting or memorable photo. It is okay to shoot a few conventional shots, but the most captivating photos are those that frame the subject in a unique or interesting way.

Give yourself more options during the selection process by taking more photos than you think you'll need. You can view your images in the camera after you have taken them to make sure you have captured a great shot, but do not spend time in the field deleting photos you don't like until after you are finished shooting. This allows you to focus on the subject or the scene instead of worrying about getting the perfect shot. Novice photographers should, at their start, focus more on composition and less on trying to shoot as much as possible. It is better to have more quality photographs than a large number of unusable photos.

Candid photos — those that are shot spontaneously without notifying the subject in advance — are the heart of breaking news photography. A photojournalist often decides within seconds what will make for an interesting photo and how to frame and shoot the image. In certain situations such as for mug shots or profile photos, it is okay to have the subject stop and pose for photographs. However, a photojournalist should not ask someone to repeat or recreate what they were just doing so they can document it in a photograph. Photojournalism aims to capture reality and fleeting moments and this approach to photography is what separates the craft from regular photography. It is not unusual for a photographer to miss a once-in-a-lifetime shot. If this happens, you should continue shooting the scene and try to be quicker the next time a can't-miss shot comes along.

Photojournalists are not only tasked with shooting photos, but also with obtaining information that can be used in *captions*, the brief bits of text that describe the scene and appear adjacent to a published photograph. Captions are usually a few descriptive sentences and must be clear, concise, and accurate. Photographers should document descriptive information about the scene, including the location or address, the date and time, and what was happening when the photograph was taken. If a person or people are the focus of the photograph, the photographer should obtain each person's name, date of birth (not just their age, which can change over time), and, optionally, a phone number that can be used to contact the subjects or to later verify information. Captions are sometimes written hours after the photograph is taken and it is better to write the information down than try to guess later which can result in inaccuracies or mistakes.

Photography can be a creative art in which the photographer recreates the scene in an artistic way, but news photography aims to represent the subject as accurately as possible. Photojournalists can and should shoot photos from creative angles or perspectives, but should avoid capturing an image in a way that alters or distorts the subject or the scene. For example, catching a person mid-sneeze or from an unflattering angle may create a more dramatic photo, but it may not accurately represent the subject. The audience, as well as the subject of the photo, can usually recognize an intentionally unflattering photo, which can in turn cause undue controversy or outrage. For example, in 2008, photographer Jill Greenberg was assigned to shoot then U.S. presidential candidate John McCain for the cover of *The Atlantic* magazine. Greenberg was criticized for intentionally lighting McCain as unflatteringly as possible, making his skin appear excessively wrinkled and his eyes appear reddish and dark. Critics accused Greenberg of allowing her own political motivation to shape her portrayal of a news subject.

Photojournalists may sometimes document subjects that make them uncomfortable, including human misery and natural disasters — subjects a non-news photographer can choose to avoid. If you don't feel comfortable shooting a photograph because of an ethical conflict, consider the moral issue at hand, but at least snap a photo or two. You can later debate whether or not to publish it, but at least you'll have a photo to consider publishing. Each situation is different so consider the newsworthiness of the subject and if the photograph will highlight or uncover an important issue or subject.

For photojournalism tips, tutorials, and resources
go to **djhandbook.net/photojournalism**

Digital photo editing

After shooting photos, photojournalists often return to the newsroom and cycle through their images to decide which photos are the best of the bunch. Before they are published, many news photos are digitally enhanced using photo editing software. Digital photo editing tools are used to increase the clarity of the image, correct the photographer's mistakes, or to optimize the photograph for print or online display. Digital software can improve photos that are too dark or too bright, enhance or alter the image's color or hue, and improve the framing of the photograph.

When it comes to photo editing software, Photoshop is the industry standard, but there are many tools that are used to digitally enhance photographs. Photoshop, a program distributed by Adobe (*www.adobe.com*), was first released in 1990 and since then has become the tool of choice for many photographers looking to improve their work. Photoshop is also used for graphic design and has many features beyond the needs of a photojournalist.

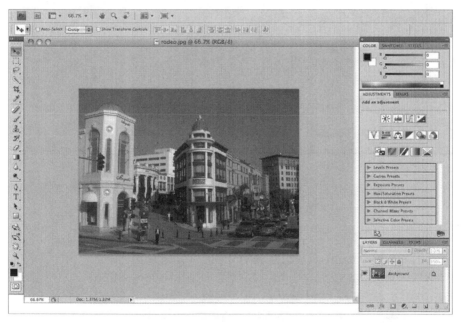

Photoshop

There are many ways photographers can enhance their images. Using photo editing software like Photoshop, photographers can crop or trim unwanted parts of an image. Photo editors can crop an image by selecting a relatively smaller portion of the photo and trimming the rest away. The crop tool is often used when the photo isn't as perfectly composed as it should be. Photographers can use the crop tool to eliminate distracting parts of the photo such as a dominating background and better frame the photograph to focus on the intended subject. When cropping photos of human beings, avoid cutting off the photo at joints such as elbows, knees, and ankles. As with framing a subject, cropping at these points can make the subject appear as if they are missing body parts. Instead, crop at portions of the body such as the chest or the middle of the thigh which creates the illusion that the body extends beyond the photo.

The photo on the right is a cropped version of the photo on the left

Cropping a photograph can create a better-framed image, but it can also change the meaning of the photo. For example, cropping an important person or element out of the photo can alter the viewer's understanding of the scene. Is it okay to crop a photo as long as it does not take away from the original meaning of the image.

Photo editing software also lets the user *rotate* or change the orientation of the photo. In Photoshop, this can be done in 90 degree increments or by using the rotate tool, which allows the editor to rotate the image freely. The rotation tool is often used to correct photos that are not right-side up, which is often caused when a photographer tilts the camera to change the framing of the photo. Digitally rotating the image can also adjust the horizon line if the photo appears askew.

Photo editors can also *resize* or change the size of an image. Most digital cameras save photos at a high level of resolution, which means they have greater detail that makes them optimal for printing. Images that appear on the web do not require the same level of detail and are often resized before they are published. Photo editors can decrease the size of a larger image and still retain

The photo on the left is rotated 90 degrees to produce the photo on the right

the clarity and crispness of the photo. However, resizing a smaller photo into a larger one can greatly reduce the quality of the photo and make the image appear blurry and distorted. This is because smaller photos have less information and detail, a problem that can only be slightly improved by digital photo editing tools.

In addition to the size of an image, photo editing software such as Photoshop can also adjust the color or hue of the photo. If, for example, the photo appears too blue, as is sometimes the case with photos taken outdoors, photo editing software can digitally add the opposite color (in this case, yellow) to balance and improve the color of the photo. Photo software can also adjust the photo's *saturation*, or the intensity of the color in the image. The more gray that is mixed in with the image's overall color, the less saturated the photo appears, which causes the image to look dull or washed-out. Photo editing software allows the user to either *saturate,* or increase the vividness of the color in a photo, or *desaturate* the photo by adding more gray, which tones down the richness of the color in an image. For example, in a heavily saturated photo of a red apple, the fruit will appear more intensely red while a desaturated photo of an apple will look more gray and lifeless. The color in a photograph can also be eliminated altogether by converting the image to *grayscale*, or a photo that contains only shades of gray, including black and white.

Photoshop and other similar photo editing tools have other useful features, including the ability to digitally enhance the level of lighting in an image. Digital editing can improve underexposed photos that are too dark and overexposed photos that are too bright or washed out. These tools can also increase the sharpness of a photo by enhancing the light and dark edges of the image to make it appear more crisp and in focus. Digital photo editing can only improve a poor photo so much — computer enhancement cannot make an intensely blurry photo appear in focus or make a dark image appear bright and well-lit. A photo with poor lighting can be digitally brightened, but the results are often spotty and unnatural. It is best to shoot good photos at the start so that they don't need to be altered with a computer program. Some photos do benefit from digital enhancement, but it is up to the photographer to decide what level of enhancement each photo requires. It takes a discerning eye and a bit of practice to recognize what can potentially be corrected in a photo, but after some time the process becomes second nature.

A little digital editing can create a clearer or more improved photo, but too much editing can take away the photo's original meaning, alter reality, or distort facts. Just as photojournalists aim to capture images that reflect reality, photo editors should use digital image editing only for minor improvements and not to intentionally alter the scene or the subject. There have been several instances where digital retouching was taken too far and changed the accuracy or original meaning of the photo. For example, in 2005, an Associated Press photo that appeared on USAToday.com showed then U.S. Secretary of State Condoleezza Rice with unusually menacing eyes, a result of too much retouching. Some critics questioned whether the effect was created deliberately because the glaring white eyes and black pupils featured in the photo could not be easily replicated using normal digital photo editing processes. The altered photo was quickly removed and replaced with a version closer to the original, along with an apology from the publication's photo editor.

In journalism, it is unethical to present a significantly altered photo as reality and is equal to intentionally misquoting an interviewee. Any digital image editing that dramatically or intentionally alters the original photo should be labeled as a "news illustration" in the caption so the audience understands the photo has been deliberately altered. Photo editors seeking to improve news photographs with digital editing software should limit enhancements to basic color or exposure correction, cropping, resizing, or conversion to grayscale.

For examples of digital photo editing, as well as tutorials and tips, go to **djhandbook.net/photoediting**

Once the photo is edited, there are several ways to save the image, depending on how it will be used or where it will appear. Most digital photos are saved as a JPG (also called JPEG) file, a digital image format used to save and store photos and display them on the web. JPGs can display up to 16 million different colors and are best suited for photographs posted online and detailed web graphics. Another popular digital image format is PNG which is comparable to JPG and is often used for online images and graphics. PNGs, however, are not compatible with some early web browsers such as Internet Explorer 6.

Many digital cameras that save photos as JPGs process and compress photos immediately after capturing them, reducing the size and level of detail in each photo. This causes a loss in quality even if the image is saved at the camera's highest quality setting. Because of this, some higher-end cameras offer photographers the option to save photos as RAW files, which leaves the image unprocessed and uncompressed. This digital format gives the photographer more control over how the camera's images are processed.

Some photographers save their images as TIFF files, a digital format that stores each image at a higher quality and with less compression than JPGs or PNGs. Images saved as TIFF files are larger and require more computer space than JPG or PNG files and can be, but are not usually, used to display images on the web. There are several other formats for saving digital images, most of which are less popular among photojournalists. Many news organizations have specific rules and guidelines on how digital images should be saved and displayed. To determine which file type you should use to save and store your images, consult your photo editor or supervisor.

AUDIO

CHAPTER FIVE

In print journalism, reporters use descriptive words and quotes from interviewees to recreate a scene or communicate a story. Instead of reading text, audio journalism allows the listener to hear the voices and experience the sounds of the story for themselves instead of relying on a reporter to accurately portray the scene. Sound can capture the voices and emotions of eyewitnesses and bring to life information that may not be communicated as well using other media. Audio journalism existed long before the web in the form of radio, a medium that continues to deliver a variety of audio-based programming and features. Now, audio journalism is no longer exclusive to radio. A variety of news media, including traditional print and television newsrooms, are producing audio content and publishing it on the web.

The web is used to present many forms of online audio journalism, including recorded interviews, meetings, discussions, or performances and extended clips of audio that were shortened to fit an on-air broadcast. Many newsrooms use audio to broadcast live or recorded dispatches from the field and to create audio-based storytelling. Online audiences can also listen to their favorite musical or non-musical radio stations on the web or catch up on individual radio programs. Unlike traditional radio that requires the audience to listen at a specific time to hear a particular program, audio programs posted to the web allow the audience to listen whenever and wherever they want. Many of the radio programs aired on NPR (*www.npr.org*), for example, are also made available online, either in whole or in part, so the listener can hear their favorite shows long after they are first broadcast. Audio is also distributed on the web in the form of *podcasts*, a series of digital audio files.

Audio can be combined with other media such as photos to create audio slideshows or can be embedded adjacent to a traditional text article to communicate a story in more than one medium. Audio can also be included in multimedia or interactive stories that combine two or more media to tell a single story. There is no limit to how audio can be used on the web and is limited only by the imagination of the journalist or producer. At the core of all these technologies and formats is high-quality audio that tells a story or shares an idea with the listener.

For examples of audio journalism
go to **djhandbook.net/audio**

Choosing an audio recorder

In today's world of digital audio and personal MP3 players, audiences are accustomed to listening to crisp, clear, and polished sound that has been carefully recorded and edited to attain the best audio quality possible. This expectation of flawless sound means journalists should also work to gather and broadcast the best audio they can. The first step to recording high-quality sound is to use a high-quality audio recorder.

Audio recorders come in many different sizes and shapes and range from inexpensive recorders with just a few features to high-end recorders with an assortment of advanced features and controls. Most audio recorders have common functions such as the ability to play, pause, record, stop, rewind, fast forward, and erase the recording. Digital audio recorders can also record individual audio *tracks* or chunks of audio. Tracks are used to separate audio clips and allow the person using the recorder to quickly locate specific portions of the audio instead of sifting through the entire recording. These audio files can later be transferred to a computer and edited individually.

A typical professional audio recorder

Some recorders feature a *time counter* that indicates how long the audio has been recording, which track is recording, and how many tracks were recorded previously. Higher-end recorders also include a graphic equalizer or meter that visualizes the audio *levels* or the volume of the sound being recorded. Levels are used to determine whether the sound is recording correctly.

Most professional audio recorders are equipped with an *input jack*, a small hole or socket used to connect the audio recorder to an external microphone. The ability to plug a microphone directly into the recorder is an essential feature necessary to obtain high-quality sound. Built-in microphones, especially those found on lower-quality recorders, cannot focus on one source of sound and instead capture all the sound around it, which is not useful for professional audio journalism. For example, recording an interview with a built-in microphone will not only pick up the sound of the person talking, but also any background noise such as passing cars, the hum of electronics, or other people talking.

There are two types of microphone connections usually found on audio recorders: TRS, also called a "mini" because of its relatively small size, and XLR, a 3-pin connector found on many professional microphones and recorders. Both TRS and XLR connections have "male" and "female" connection points. The "male" input jack is found at the end of the microphone cable and is inserted into the female end found on the recorder.

TRS, short for "tip, ring, sleeve," is a common audio connector usually found on consumer-level headphones and audio players such as the iPod. TRS describes the three contact points: the tip is the contact point at the end of the jack, the contact point next to it is the ring and the longest contact is the sleeve. TRS connectors are available in 1/4" (0.635 cm) and 1/8" (0.3175 cm) diameter models.

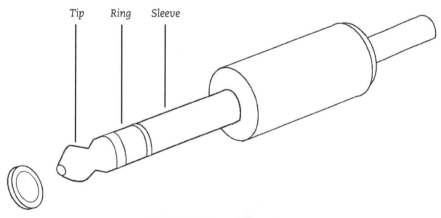

A typical TRS connection system

Instead of a single jack, an XLR connection has three pins arranged in a triangle. The pins are aligned and inserted into three corresponding holes on the audio recorder or other electronic equipment. XLR jacks are more rugged and lock into place, which is useful for recording in the field or other situations where the recorder is moving. TRS input jacks can easily slip out of the audio recorder or produce a rustling sound if the jack is moved during the recording.

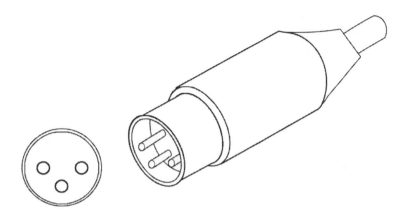

A typical XLR connection system

There are several ways that audio recorders save and store audio. Some recorders have built-in hard drives that allow the user to store audio directly to the recorder. The audio is transferred from the recorder to a computer using a cable. There are two common types of cable connection systems: USB and FireWire. USB, short for Universal Serial Bus, is a system for connecting a computer to electronic equipment such as an audio recorder. USB is standard on modern computers and is also used to connect many other electronic devices such as photo and video cameras.

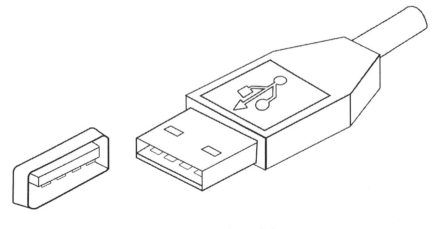

A USB connection and plug

FireWire is another system used to transfer information between a computer and electronic equipment. A FireWire connection can transfer more data at higher speeds than a USB cable and is standard on most newer Mac computers and laptops.

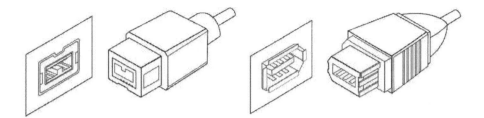

A FireWire 400 port and plug; a FireWire 800 port and plug, two common FireWire connections

To transfer audio from a recorder using a cable, connect one end of the USB or FireWire cable to the recorder and the other to the computer. Once the recorder is connected, a folder containing the audio files appears on the computer. These files can be transferred to another location on the computer or stored on the audio recorder's hard drive. For more information, consult the manual included with the recorder.

Some audio recorders use *memory cards* to store audio files. Memory cards are flat, removable disks about the size of a large postage stamp and are inserted into a dedicated slot on the recorder. Memory cards vary in thickness and transfer speed and are available from a variety of manufacturers.

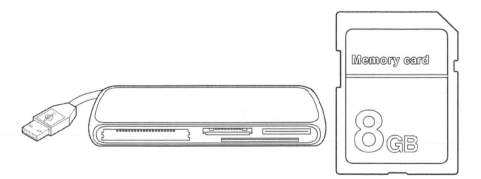

A *memory card reader (left) and memory card (enlarged to show detail)*

Memory cards are reusable and can also be used to store photos and other digital media. Digital files stored on memory cards are transferred to a computer using a memory card reader, a small external drive connected to the computer. Memory card readers are purchased separately from the audio recorder.

MiniDiscs, which are similar to the floppy disks of yesteryear, are another format for storing high-quality audio. Each disc is encased in a protective shell 2.75 inches (7 cm) wide, 2.65 inches (6.75 cm) high, and 0.2 inches (0.5 cm) deep and can store up to 80 minutes of digital audio. MiniDiscs can be used many times and still retain the same quality as the first recording. Audio files recorded on a MiniDisc are transferred to a computer using either a USB or FireWire cable, depending on the model of the recorder.

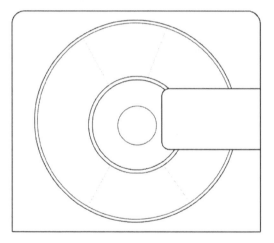

A MiniDisc

The type of audio recorder you select should be based on your budget as well as how much audio you plan to record. No matter which recorder you choose, it should be equipped with a jack to connect an external microphone and a way to easily transfer the recorded audio to a computer. It is a common misconception that audio that will be published on the web can be recorded with a cheaper recorder and that only broadcast-quality audio requires a more advanced recorder. This is not true. More inexpensive recorders produce lower quality audio and some add an audible hum or hiss that makes the audio unusable. Web audiences, more so than television or radio listeners, are often listening with headphones and are more likely to notice inferior audio.

Journalists should use digital recorders instead of models that use tapes or cassettes. These models can only record a single stream of audio, cannot create separate audio files, and record audio that cannot be easily transferred to a computer. Transcription and tape recorders should only be used for personal notes or dictation. Some digital recorders require the user to transfer the audio to the computer in real-time. This means that for every minute of audio you record, you will have to wait a minute for the audio to transfer to the computer, a slow process that can be avoided altogether. In addition, stay away from recorders that only record in WMA (Windows Media Audio) or other proprietary formats that require additional conversion software to use, which adds more time to the audio editing process.

Before heading out into the field, read the manual included with your recorder and become familiar with its functions, features, and buttons and how to access them quickly. The ability to operate an audio recorder without actually looking at it is a valuable skill that can save time and make on-the-spot recording even easier.

Microphones and accessories

A professional microphone is as important to audio recording as the recorder itself and is an essential part of an audio journalist's tool kit. There are many different types of microphones, each of which has specific uses. The most common type of microphone is a *handheld* mic, a catchall term for a microphone that can be held in the palm of the hand. Microphones are also categorized by their *pickup pattern*, or the direction in which sound enters the microphone.

Omnidirectional or *multi-directional* microphones pick up sound equally from all directions and are useful for capturing many speakers in a single room or for recording background sound. These microphones should not be used to target and record a specific source of sound. In addition to the target, omnidirectional microphones also capture all the sounds around the subject. For example, if you record an interview in a noisy room with an omnidirectional mic, the microphone will not only pick up the voice of the interviewee, but also any noise around them, which creates muddled and unusable audio.

A *unidirectional* microphone picks up sound from one direction only — usually the front of the mic — and is less likely to pick up unwanted background noise. Unidirectional mics are useful for capturing isolated sounds such as an interview with a single person or to focus on one particular sound. A unidirectional microphone must be pointed directly at the source or the microphone will not pick up the sound and will transmit lower quality audio to the recorder.

A *cardioid* microphone is a common type of directional microphone with a heart-shaped pickup pattern. Unlike a regular unidirectional mic, a cardioid mic picks up sound at the front of the mic and a little less sound from the sides.

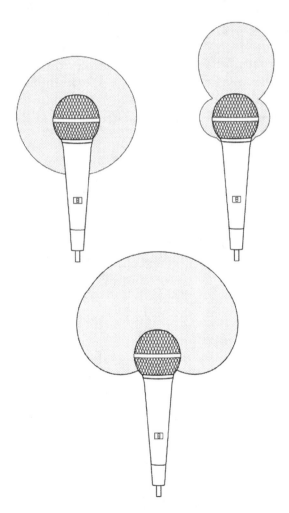

(Clockwise, from top left) An omnidirectional pickup patterm; a unidirectional pickup pattern; a cardioid pickup pattern

A *shotgun* microphone, another type of directional mic, records sound that enters the front of the microphone and is less sensitive on the sides and rear. A shotgun mic is longer than other microphones and can pick up sound from longer distances which allows the person holding the mic to stand further away from the subject. Shotgun mics can be held in the hand or at the end of a special pole called a *boom*. In journalism, booms are often used when there is an additional person responsible for recording the sound. This person positions the microphone at the end of the boom and above or near the subject while the reporter or cameraperson conducts the interview.

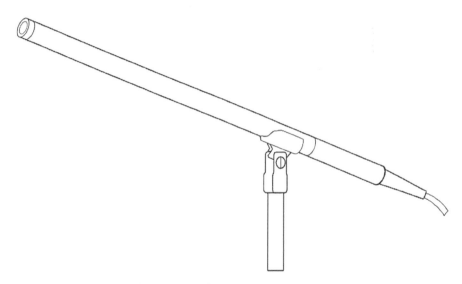

A typical shotgun microphone positioned on a boom

A *lavalier*, also called a *lav* or *lapel mic*, is a type of microphone that is small and worn on the body instead of held in the hand. Lavalier mics are either attached to a cord that is directly connected to the recorder or are wireless. A wireless lavalier has two parts: the first part consists of a small microphone attached to a transmitter by a thin cord. The microphone end is fastened to the subject's clothing using a small clip and the wireless transmitter on the other end is usually clipped to the subject's belt or pocket. The second part of the wireless lav is a receiver that is connected directly to the recorder and receives the audio signal from the microphone. Wireless lavalier mics allow the interviewee to walk or gesture freely because the microphone's cord is not directly attached to the recorder. Wireless lavs also free the reporter's hands and can make the interviewee feel more at ease than they would with a microphone in their face.

Lavaliers are also used during video interviews and are usually clipped to the body in a way that keeps the microphone out of the view of the camera. The microphone end of the lavalier is clipped to the subject's clothing, usually above the chest but under the chin, either on the lapel of a suit jacket, the front of a necktie, or to a button-up shirt. If the lavalier is attached to a shirt or blouse, the cord is usually threaded under the shirt and through an opening to keep the cord hidden from the camera and only the small microphone visible. This position allows the microphone to be close to the subject's mouth and the rest of the mic, including the cord and the transmitter, hidden from view. Avoid placing a lavalier where it will rub against the subject's clothing and ask the interviewee to remove any noisy jewelry such as necklaces or earrings which can cause noisy and unusable audio.

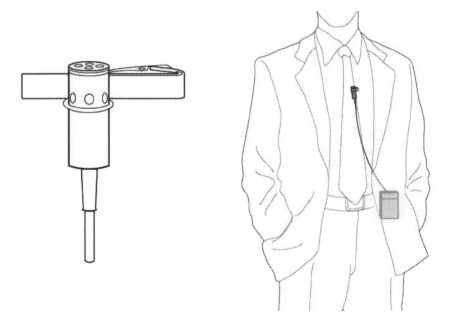

(left) A typical lavalier mic with a clip attached; a lavalier mic clipped to a necktie and attached to a transmitter clipped to the waist

Like a lavalier mic, some microphones operate wirelessly and are powered by a battery while others are powered by an XLR cable connected to the audio recorder or other electronic device. The type of microphone you use for each recording should depend on the speaker or source of audio and the surrounding environment. Microphones may have similar pickup patterns, but can range in price and quality. Before using your microphone in the field, you should first test its quality and how it picks up sound.

The position of the microphone is essential to obtaining the best recording possible. For audio interviews, most handheld directional microphones should be positioned 6 to 12 inches (15 to 30 cms) away from the speaker and pointed directly at his or her mouth. If the microphone is too close, the audio will become distorted. If it is too far, the microphone is more likely to pick up unwanted background noise.

A microphone positioned to capture the speaker's voice

Some interviewees aren't familiar with the proper way to hold or use a microphone and naturally move it away from their mouth, which can create an inconsistent audio recording. For example, if an interviewee turns their head away from the microphone, the recorder will not pick up the sound and will instead record poor audio or noticeably different audio levels. Whenever possible, the reporter should hold the microphone to maintain control over the audio and the interview.

Reporters should also avoid holding the recorder or microphone during lengthy interviews for the same reason. The human hand can naturally become shaky and unsteady, creating inconsistent audio levels. Reporters can sometimes use a *microphone stand*, a device that provides support for the microphone. A mic stand is an adjustable telescoping tube or series of tubes with a cradle on one end to hold the microphone. Mic stands range from tabletop models to floor models, and are more often used in pre-planned interviews where the subject will not move.

Another essential tool for professional audio recording is a high-quality pair of headphones. Headphones should always be worn during audio recording to monitor the sound and ensure that the best quality audio is recorded. Nothing is worse than gathering once-in-a-lifetime audio, listening to it later, and discovering something was wrong with the recorder or the microphone. Reporters can avoid this situation by wearing headphones at all times. Audio journalists should ideally use noise-canceling headphones so the recording can be heard clearly. Most inexpensive earbuds like those that come with portable audio players like the iPod don't offer a full spectrum of audio and cannot be heard easily in a noisy environment. Better isolation allows you to more accurately gauge the quality of your audio.

 For a guide to commonly used audio recorders and accessories, go to **djhandbook.net/audiorecorders**

Recording in the field

Before you head out into the field to record your audio, make sure you are equipped with a fully charged audio recorder, a pair of headphones, the necessary microphones, and additional equipment such as memory cards, cables, and extra batteries. When you arrive at the scene and before you begin the actual recording, test the levels of your audio by listening through the headphones and, if your recorder is equipped with a graphic equalizer or other visual gauge, monitor it to determine that the audio is recording at an appropriate level. It is better to consult the recorder's graphic equalizer instead of the volume you hear in your headphones, because the headphone volume level can often be adjusted separately from the volume of the sound being recorded. The recording may sound perfect, but it may not represent the actual audio levels.

The volume of the sound that enters the microphone should be loud enough to obtain a quality recording, but not so high that the audio becomes distorted. If a recording is too quiet, it can sometimes be improved with digital editing. However, distorted audio caused by recording sound at too loud a volume cannot be digitally corrected. If you know the sound you plan to record will be loud, pull the microphone further away from the source.

Once you begin recording, double-check that the record button is on and, if it has one, that the recorder's timer is running. In every new setting, you should first record 30 seconds of *room tone*, or what sounds like silence, but actually contains sound that may go unnoticed by an inattentive ear. Each room has a particular sound profile and contains faints sounds such as the hum of a refrigerator or the buzz of nearby vehicle traffic. Room tone can be used in the editing process to cover gaps in the recording. For example, if an interviewee coughs in the middle of a thought, instead of just cutting out the cough and leaving absolute silence, the interruption can be covered with room tone that matches the same "silence" heard in the pauses and gaps of the conversation.

In addition to room tone, you should also record *preroll* and *postroll* or a few seconds before and after your actual recording. Audio editing tools sometimes require extra space to create effects such as transitions and fades. Recording preroll and postroll for each track gives editing software the space necessary to create these effects.

Whenever possible, record in a quiet space free from audible distractions that can lower the quality of the audio. To reduce or eliminate unwanted noise, close nearby windows and doors and unplug unnecessary electronics and appliances. This keeps the background sound from overwhelming or distracting from the main source of audio. Also, avoid recording sounds unique to journalists such as the click of a photographer's camera or scribbling on a notepad, which can easily be picked up by a recorder.

Recording sound outdoors can present its own problems. Wind can cause audible rumbling and whooshing sounds that cannot be reduced or eliminated with digital audio editing software, rendering audio unusable. Most microphones are equipped with or have an optional *windscreen*, a spherical piece of foam or special material that covers the microphone and reduces the noise created by wind. Windscreens can also combat *plosives* and *sibilance*, or the small boom created when a person speaking too close to a microphone says a "P" or "B" sound (plosive) or an "S" sound (sibilance). These distracting sounds are caused when air expelled from the lungs creates a small burst of wind that is picked up by the microphone. Plosives and sibilance temporarily overload the mic and can distort the recording.

 To hear examples of poor audio, including wind noise, plosives, and sibilance, go to **djhandbook.net/badaudio**

It is important to record the best audio possible instead of trying to improve it later with digital editing, which can add unnecessary time to a project. In addition, you should only record what you need to tell your story. If you record an hour of audio, you will likely spend an hour or more listening to that audio again during the editing process. You can also reduce time spent editing by creating separate audio tracks for different scenes, interviews, or when a single interview shifts gears. This will lessen the time necessary to later locate a specific portion of the audio. Keeping a log of what you record can also make locating and editing audio easier. Write notes describing what you have recorded, as well as the track number or the time in the recording where it appears. This log can be referred to later when you begin assembling your audio clips.

Audio Session #1	
0:00 – 1:34	Interview with Jane Smith
1:35 – 4:57	Interview with Mick Jones
4:58 – 6:10	Audio of children playing
6:11 – 6:42	Cows mooing in barn

An audio log

Audio recording is often done in combination with several other tasks such as writing notes or shooting photos for multimedia stories. It is difficult, but not impossible to handle an audio recorder, a notepad, and a camera at the same time, but juggling multiple tools means you will sometimes miss great audio or will be unable to shoot a great photograph. It is up to the individual journalist to decide what moment will make for great audio and when to set down the camera or the notepad.

Interviewing

Interviews play a major role in all forms of journalism, but especially audio journalism. Reporters often use recorded interviews to let the audience listen to the speaker express themselves and use recorded comments to support audio news stories. Journalists who document stories with audio conduct interviews much in the same way a print reporter would, asking questions that elicit thoughts and emotions from the interviewee. The difference is the audience can hear the emotion instead of just reading about it.

Before you begin recording and even before you pick up the audio recorder, take a minute to talk with the interviewee and get a feel for their voice, whether they talk softly or loudly, and whether you need to adjust the recorder or microphone. Before you begin the actual interview, conduct a soundcheck to gauge the audio quality and that the speaker's voice is recorded properly. Ask a question that encourages the interviewee to speak naturally such as "What did you do today?" or "What did you have for breakfast?" This type of question is better than "Testing, 1, 2, 3" or similar phrases because asking an actual question encourages the speaker to talk in their natural voice. As they speak, check the audio levels on the recorder and listen through your headphones to make sure you can hear the person clearly.

This brief period before the interview can also make the interviewee feel more at ease. Some people become nervous when a microphone is in their face, so if the speaker looks anxious, talk with them a little first so they speak naturally once the interview begins. Once you begin recording the actual interview, have the speaker first say and spell out their name and title so you can transcribe it later.

Because the interviewer is often edited out of the final recording, you should encourage the interviewee to speak in complete sentences that will make sense to an audience who will not hear the original question. "Yes" and "no" answers do not work for audio journalism, except in interviews where the entire conversation is included in the recording. Instead, ask open-ended questions that will encourage a longer answer. For example, "How was your day?" will elicit a more complete response than "Did you have a good day?" which will likely result in a "yes" or "no" answer. If the interviewee speaks in complete sentences, the interviewer can be edited from the final audio piece and the listening audience will still understand the speaker's response.

Try to keep the interviewee from rambling and their answers short, which creates better, more concise audio, but do not cut the interviewee off. Allow the speaker to complete his or her sentences and do not interrupt unless it is absolutely necessary. It is natural to want to verbally respond to the person's answer as you would in an ordinary conversation. However, in audio journalism, the sound of a reporter audibly responding or talking over an interviewee as he or she is speaking is both distracting to the listener and difficult to edit. Instead, practice non-verbal cues: nod, don't talk, and use your hands to communicate with the person as they speak.

Don't be afraid to ask the interviewee to repeat themselves if their statement is ever unclear or inaudible. Otherwise, that portion of the audio cannot be used and will be edited out. Listen and ask follow-up questions while keeping an eye on the recorder and the audio levels, but also try to look directly at the person, not the equipment. If the interviewee sees you looking at the recorder, he or she can become more conscious that they are being recorded or determine that you are not listening. In both cases, the interviewee may become less likely to answer questions.

Sometimes it is necessary to record interviews over the phone if the person isn't able to be interviewed in person. Journalists can use special recording devices available at major electronic stores or internet telephone services such as Google Voice (*www.google.com/voice*) to record phone interviews. These tools can be used to create editable digital audio files. Before you begin a telephone interview, you should first let the caller know that they are being recorded. In some areas of the world, it is illegal to record a phone conversation without the other person's knowledge. Often, the quality of a phone interview is audibly inferior to an in-person interview and has a noticeable tone that indicates it was conducted over the phone. Mention this to your listeners either before the audio clip or in a paragraph of text posted on the web adjacent to the audio.

The same rules apply for phone interviews as they do for in-person interviews: avoid talking over the person and allow him or her to finish their thought.

Ambient sound

Every good audio story depends on strong characters and voices to communicate the story. In addition to interviews or recorded comments, many audio journalism pieces also include *ambient sound,* the natural sounds that are present in a scene. Also called *raw sound, natural sound,* or *nat sound,* this type of audio lets the listener hear the sounds that represent the scene and is similar to a writer using descriptive words to recreate a story. For example, an audio piece about a doctor could include natural sounds heard in a hospital such as the beeping of machinery, the buzz of an intercom or the sound of gurneys wheeled down a hallway. These background sounds send aural cues to the listener that the story is set in a hospital. Instead of having someone talk about what they do, you can record them actually do it. For example, instead of simply recording an interview with a teacher discussing his or her profession, you can also record the teacher in the classroom talking to students. This type of ambient sound can accompany an interview in the final piece.

Ambient sound should be recorded separately from interviews and blended later in the editing process. While interviews and ambient sound can physically be recorded at the same time, often one overwhelms the other, creating muddled audio. Recording these sounds separately creates cleaner audio and greater flexibility in the editing process. Also, recording ambient sound from a distance can create unclear audio that is difficult for the listener to understand. Instead of just sticking a microphone in the air and hoping for the best, get close to the source of the sound and focus your audio recording. Ambient sound should be collected in the same session as other elements of the story and should be representative of the scene and the subject. For example, it is not fair to record a troubled politician and digitally add the slam of a prison door recorded at a separate time or location. Except in rare circumstances, do not attempt to recreate sounds later or use sound effects in your audio story. This is ethically wrong and is equal to including fabricated information in a print story.

Narration

An audio story should ideally be told using the voices of key players and witnesses or using ambient sound to recreate the scene. Sometimes *narration*, a voiceover recorded by the reporter or other speaker that recounts the action, is necessary to complete the story. Narration is often used to summarize a story, fill in gaps in the recording, or as an introduction to an audio story. It also used for first person accounts of news events or as the audio equivalent of a newspaper column where the reporter offers his or her opinion on a given topic or subject.

Professional narration should be recorded in a soundproof, echo-free room that facilitates high-quality audio recording. Professional soundbooths like those found in broadcast newsrooms can be very expensive to build and are usually outfitted with special acoustic padding and audio equipment used to achieve the best sound possible. The average non-broadcast newsroom often doesn't have access to a soundbooth or can't afford such a pricey setup. A professional soundbooth can be replicated somewhat by recording narration in a closet or small room and hanging blankets on the walls, which reduces echo and outside interference.

Before you record your narration, you should first write a script that you can read as you record, which lessens the chance that you will stumble over your words. The script should be double-spaced and printed in a font large enough for the narrator to read comfortably without straining to see the words. The script should be written in a natural, conversational tone that sounds as if you are speaking to the listener, not reading to them. This style of writing is familiar to broadcast journalists, but is the opposite of traditional newspaper writing. Talking "naturally" doesn't actually come naturally and takes conscious effort and practice. Pretend you are telling the story to a friend as you write your script. Your narration will sound more like a conversation and less like someone reading a story.

Practice reading the script a few times before you record it to familiarize yourself with what you are about to say. Take a moment to look for complicated words or phrases that may cause you to stumble. Any words you have trouble reading aloud can be spelled out phonetically so you can read the word with ease. Add marks to the script where you will pause, stop, or add emphasis. These notes will keep you from turning the page into a long run-on sentence.

Story Narration

WALL-LOW-WITS
Peter Wolowicz always wanted his own

pause
car, but could never afford the high

payments. His dream <u>finally</u> came true

Thursday after he won the lottery. The

WOO-STER
thirty one year old man from Worcester

A script with notes added to it

A narrator should speak in a tone that is appropriate for the topic. Reading an obituary with an upbeat voice, for example, counteracts the tone of the story. For most news stories, the narrator's tone should be authoritative, but conversational. To achieve this, you should stand, not sit, as you record narration. Sitting makes the voice sound relaxed and standing gives the voice more alertness and authority.

When recording narration, make sure you aren't talking too fast and enunciate words so they can be heard clearly and accurately. A common mistake most novice narrators make is rushing through the script. Eliminate a hurried tone in your voice by exhaling before each recording and taking a breath at the end of sentences. Avoid taking breaths in the middle of a sentence or thought, which is distracting to the listener. Breaths taken after a sentence can be digitally edited out, but a listener can easily tell if the narrator is holding his or her breath while reading the copy.

Count down each take before you record it so the audio editor knows where to begin or end a clip. Record a few seconds of silence before and after each take just as you would when recording in the field. If you stumble or make a mistake while reading the script, leave a noticeable pause and repeat the entire sentence. Do not start again at the last word you spoke before you stumbled because even if the audio is edited and the mistake is removed, there will still be a noticeable difference in your voice before and after the gap. It is okay to record multiple takes because it gives the editor more options to choose from. Narration should, however, be recorded in a single session. Your voice can fluctuate from day to day, which causes noticeable changes in the audio. For example, if you are upbeat one day and tired the next, listeners will be able to hear the difference in your voice.

Great narration comes with practice. Record and listen to yourself and look for ways that you can improve your technique. Over time, recording narration should come naturally.

 For examples of good and bad audio narration
go to **djhandbook.net/narration**

Audio editing

Just like a text story is edited before it is printed, audio should be edited before it is broadcast or published on the web. Audio is edited to delete mistakes or unwanted audio or to assemble various audio clips into a single narrative. One of the most common reasons audio is edited is to shorten the length of a longer clip. An audio story or file that is posted to the web should be relatively short, usually no longer than a few minutes. This will help keep the listener's attention. There are a few exceptions such as lengthy audio programs, whole interviews, podcasts, and online broadcasts. No matter the length of the audio or how it is used, the audio should be interesting enough to listen from beginning to end.

While there are some newsrooms where the recorder or audio files are handed over to another staff member such as an audio editor or web producer for editing, many journalists are required to both record and edit their own audio. Editing the audio you record has its advantages: you know what was recorded and where the best parts of the audio are. Handing over an audio file to someone else takes longer because they don't know what happened or what was recorded. Therefore, it is important for journalists to be familiar with the audio editing process.

In the early days of audio, sound was edited by recording one audio clip after the other to another source, until the second source contained all the necessary audio clips. This process is called *linear editing* because the audio is edited in a single line, starting at the beginning of the audio and continuing until the audio piece is finished. Linear editing allows little room for mistakes. The editor cannot go back and rearrange the audio without starting over from the beginning. In the digital era, audio is edited using *non-linear* editing software, a computer program or system used to digitally mix and manipulate audio. Digital editing software allows the user to record and edit audio in any order he or she chooses, as well as layer multiple tracks on top of each other and create special audio effects. Digitally editing audio is similar to cutting, copying, and pasting text in a word processing program like Microsoft Word. However, instead of cutting and pasting words, an audio editor cuts, copies, and pastes audio clips to create a story.

There are various software used for editing audio, some of which are less complex and cater to novice users and others that have different features and functions that professional audio editors require. Some of the most popular audio editing tools among journalists are Audacity, GarageBand, Pro Tools, and Adobe Audition.

Audacity (*audacity.sourceforge.net*) is free digital audio editing software that can be used to record live audio directly to the computer and edit a seemingly unlimited number of audio tracks in a single project. The program has a variety of tools for enhancing audio, including noise removal and hiss reduction. Audacity is easy to use and is great for novice audio editors. The program is available for both Windows and Mac computers.

GarageBand (*www.apple.com/ilife/garageband*) was created for editing music and podcasts, but many journalists use the program to edit audio projects. Like Audacity, audio editors can use GarageBand to record and edit multiple tracks of audio and apply special effects. Unlike Audacity, GarageBand includes features specifically for creating podcasts and original music. The program is bundled with music clips that can be included in an audio project. GarageBand users can also add photos, links to online content, and chapter markers to audio to create enhanced podcasts. The audio editing program is included with all newer Mac computers as part of the system's iLife package. The bundle also includes other multimedia programs such as iPhoto, used for browsing and editing images, and iMovie, which is used to edit video. GarageBand is not available for PCs.

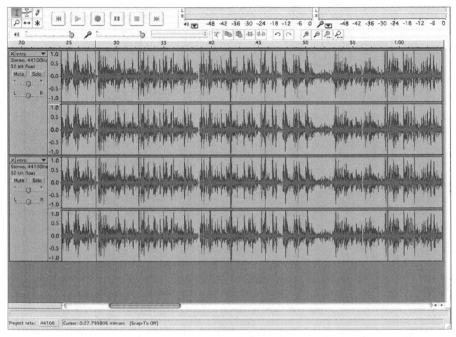

Audacity

GarageBand

Pro Tools (*www.digidesign.com*) and Adobe Audition (*www.adobe.com/products/ audition*), two professional audio editing programs, have the same basic features as Audacity, but also come with advanced audio editing tools and a higher price tag than their free counterparts. Pro Tools, a program available for both Windows and Mac computers, is a popular choice among professionals in the music, film, and television industry. The software has many features that professionals need and use, but also has a steep learning curve that can overwhelm the novice editor. Audition, distributed by Adobe, is a comprehensive audio editing program with an interface similar to Audacity, but has advanced features and audio enhancement tools used for professional audio editing. Audition is more novice-friendly and easier to learn than Pro Tools.

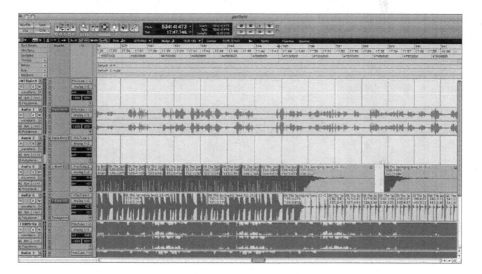

Pro Tools

The audio editing program you use should depend on your audio editing experience and whether you need advanced features to construct your project. Audacity and GarageBand can handle simple audio editing, but professional audio editors may find the programs don't suit their needs. Many audio journalists prefer one editing program over the other, but you should determine for yourself which one is best for you. A novice video editor should start with a free program like Audacity, explore its capabilities, and become familiar with basic audio editing. If you find you need more advanced features, you can upgrade to a more advanced program.

Most audio editing programs, including those just mentioned, share the same basic structure and layout. Audio is imported into the program and placed on a *timeline*, a visual representation of the sequence of the audio. The timeline can contain multiple layers called *tracks* that are stacked one on top of the other. Each track can contain one or more audio clips.

Each audio clip appears as a *waveform*, a visual representation of an audio recording that shows the changes in volume over the span of the clip. The *amplitude* or volume of the audio is measured vertically while time is measured horizontally. The taller the spike in the waveform, the louder the sound and the longer the waveform, the longer the audio clip. For example, if a speaker spoke loudly, paused, and began talking again, the waveform would begin with a large spike, followed by a short plateau, followed by another spike in the waveform. A waveform does not indicate how the audio "sounds."

A *waveform*

One of the most useful skills an audio editor can have is the ability to "read" a waveform. With a bit of experience, you'll be able to look at a waveform and predict what kind of sound it represents and more quickly recognize significant changes in the audio. This skill will also enable you to identify the part of the recording you want to edit. Audio editing at its core is the act of moving and editing waveforms.

A waveform can be dragged to different locations on the timeline, rearranged, and edited. Audio editors can cut, split (also called *splice*), or trim the audio to get rid of unwanted pauses or mistakes and copy and paste audio clips or whole waveforms. These edits are made using a *playhead* or *scrubber* (the terms are sometimes used interchangeably), a line that the editor uses to indicate where to start playing audio or where to make a cut. The line that stretches vertically across the timeline is sometimes referred to as the scrubber, while the marker on top of the scrubber is the playhead. The scrubber is also used as a selection tool to highlight or select portions of audio. Audio editors also feature buttons to record, play, rewind, and fast forward audio files and a time counter to indicate the progression of the audio.

 To see a digital audio editing program in action
go to **djhandbook.net/audioediting**

Before you begin editing your audio, listen to what you recorded or consult your audio log and write notes on what clips you'd like to include in your audio story. Often you will record much more audio than you will include in the final piece. Listen for *soundbites*, short phrases or sentences from a longer interview or recording that capture the essence of what the speaker or interviewee has said. Just as a newspaper or broadcast story includes only the best quotes, select the soundbites that best tell the story or contribute to the narrative. Decide on a tentative order for your audio story by creating a script that outlines what audio clips should appear where. You can refer to this script once you begin selecting and editing your audio files.

To begin editing, connect your audio recorder to the computer and locate your audio files. Each recorder is different, so consult the instructions found in the manual included with the recorder to find out how to access your files. Complex audio projects can contain a large number of audio files. To make the editing process easier, place all your audio files in one folder on your computer so they are easily accessible. Most audio editing can be done from a regular computer hard drive, but for complex audio editing consider using an *external hard drive* to store large audio files. An external hard drive, a portable storage system connected to the computer using a USB or FireWire connection, is used to store large files such as audio or video files. Instead of editing your original audio files, save a copy of each file, either on the computer or other drive, and use the copies to build your audio piece. If you edit and save an audio file and find you've made an irreparable mistake, you will still have the original file to work from.

Once you identify what the final audio piece should sound like, assemble the audio clips on the timeline using your script as a guide. The clips may come from separate recordings or even different points in the audio, but should be edited and arranged to create a single narrative that the listener can follow. Like a print story, audio stories should have a strong narrative — a beginning, middle, and end — and the clips should form a complete story. Ambient sound can be included in an audio project to set the scene, create transition between speakers, or layered on top of other audio clips. The ambient sound should complement the project and should contribute to the story and not distract from it.

Music is sometimes added to audio as an intro or outro to an audio piece or if the subject of the story is a musician or performer. It is sometimes tempting to include the latest Top 40 record or some other piece of copyrighted music or audio to enhance the piece. However, including even just a few seconds of copyrighted material may present a legal issue. Copyright laws vary from country to country, but in many cases, including protected works in an audio piece, even in the name of journalism, can be grounds for a lawsuit. If you plan to include copyrighted material in your piece, first consult a lawyer to determine what you can and can't use or, better yet, just leave it out.

Music is also used to create drama or underscore the emotion of a piece. Opinions vary on whether this ethical or not: while music can set the tone of a story, it can also alter the listener's emotional response and function as a subtle form of bias. Either way, music should not overpower the speaker and should be placed on a separate track at a lower volume. Audio editing programs allow users to raise or lower the volume of separate tracks and lowering the volume of the music or ambient sound ensures that the speaker is heard clearly.

Save for a few exceptions, your final audio piece should be relatively short. Many online listeners are impatient and would prefer to listen to short soundbites taken from an hour-long speech than listen to the entire speech for an hour. If a recording is long, it should be edited into separate audio clips that are more easily digestible. Keep your audio short and the listener interested by editing out obvious repetition, or the same idea repeated more than once by the same person or multiple people. If a point is made once, it is usually not necessary to repeat it again.

In addition to removing unnecessary audio clips, audio editors often eliminate or reduce distracting elements such as long pauses, mumbling, or convoluted statements. Ums and ahs, pauses, breaths, and stutters can offer insight into the speaker's personality and speech pattern, but can also be jarring to the listener and make the audio longer. Removing these indicators is ultimately altering a person's natural voice and the decision of whether to do so depends on the editor's personal judgment or the newsroom's style. It is okay to rearrange parts of an audio clip or interview for clarity, but do not alter the audio in a way that will change the meaning or context in which something was said. Editing a speaker to alter the speaker's original words or thoughts is equal to intentionally misquoting a source and should be done only in rare circumstances.

Hums or hisses heard in the background of an audio recording are sometimes digitally reduced so the sound is as clear as possible. Programs like Audacity and Audition have built-in tools for digitally reducing this extra noise. Often this is done by using a sample of room tone. The audio editor identifies the room tone in the recording and, using a digital tool, the range of sounds found in the room tone is eliminated from the entire audio file. This form of enhancement can make the audio clearer and less noisy. Digitally eliminating background sounds from an audio clip can produce mixed results and you should consult the program's user manual for further instruction. Digitally altering an audio recording sometimes presents ethical issues and journalists should find a balance between enhancing audio quality and altering a scene or interview in an unethical way.

The key to editing great audio is to simply listen to make sure that the piece tells a clear story and that the final clip is free from mistakes or other distractions. Always use headphones when you edit so you can hear the audio clearly. Some distracting elements like background noise, wind, or hiss can go unnoticed without them. Once you finish editing your piece, close your eyes and listen to your audio. If something sounds wrong, if a person is talking too long, if the sounds are overwhelming each other, or there are other inconsistent elements, identify the problem and fix it. If the audio was recorded poorly and cannot be digitally enhanced, throw it out instead of trying to salvage it. Listeners will not sit through bad audio, with few exceptions.

Audio editing becomes easier with practice so the more you do it, the better you'll become. Start by recording your interviews or other audio elements while in the field and create audio news stories with the clips. If you practice editing audio in your spare time, you will be able to edit and arrange your audio faster when you do it in a professional setting.

For audio editing tutorials and resources
go to **djhandbook.net/audioediting**

Posting and sharing audio

Once your audio file is edited, it should be saved in one of a few common audio file formats. There are many different types of audio files — the most popular among digital journalists are MP3, a compressed audio format, and WAV, used for uncompressed sound. Compression refers to the amount of data in an audio file. To create a compressed audio file, information is stripped from the file to create a smaller file size, though there is often no audible difference after compression. For example, if you save an audio file as an MP3, the size of the audio file is reduced, which makes it load faster when it is published on the web. A WAV file, on the other hand, is not compressed and contains more data and has better audio quality than an MP3 file. Other audio file formats include WMA, a compressed digital audio format developed by Windows, AIFF, an uncompressed format developed by Apple, and M4A, a compressed audio format also developed by Apple, all of which are less often used for audio and multimedia production.

The easiest way to make audio available online is to simply upload the file to the web and create a link to the file. Depending on the format of the file, the web browser will automatically create an audio player that allows the audience to listen to the file. However, online audio is more commonly made available through an *embedded audio player*. Embedded audio players are so named because they can be embedded in various types of websites alongside other content or media. Audio players have common functions such as the ability to play, pause, stop, and adjust the volume of the audio, and can include a timeline that identifies the progression and total time of the audio file. These players are usually created using Flash, the animation software outlined in Chapter 10.

For step-by-step tutorials on how to create and embed an audio player go to **djhandbook.net/audioplayer**

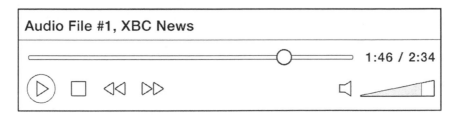

The layout of a typical embedded audio player

Many online news sites have their own proprietary audio players or specific ways to upload audio to the web, so consult your newsroom's web producer or site manager for more information. If you don't have access to an embeddable audio player, sites like SoundCloud (*www.soundcloud.com*) allow anyone to upload and store audio files and embed them on the web.

Many embedded audio players contain *streaming audio* or online audio that can be listened to immediately without waiting for the audio file to download. There are two main types of streaming audio: *on demand* where the audio file is stored online and available to be streamed when the listener accesses the player and *live streaming* where the listener "tunes in" to audio broadcast live on the web. Online audio can also be presented in combination with other media such as photos to create audio slideshows or combined with Flash to create multimedia and interactive stories.

No matter how audio is presented on the web, it should be accompanied by a text summary that describes what the listener will hear or, alternatively, a transcription of the audio. Summaries and transcriptions help online visitors decide if the clip is something they want to listen to. Text descriptions also optimize audio files so they can be found by search engines like Google that cannot "hear" or index the content of the audio. A summary should include keywords that describe the content of the audio file, which in turn helps search engine users find your clip.

Podcasting

Radio has long been a destination for audio series such as talk shows and news programming. *Podcasts,* a series of syndicated digital audio or other media files distributed over the internet, have freed audio programs from the confines of radio. Podcasts allow anyone to create and share a recorded audio series using the internet as a platform for distribution. The word "podcast" is a combination of "iPod" and "broadcast" — signifying that podcasts are often played on portable MP3 players like the iPod. An iPod, however, is not required to listen to a podcast. The audio files can be downloaded from the web and listened to either on a computer or using a digital audio device such as a portable audio player. The listener can decide when and where they want to listen to a podcast, as well as pause and restart the podcast at any time.

Podcasts are very similar to blogs: they span a range of subjects — from news to sports to politics and everything in between — and sometimes focus on topics that cater to a very specific audience. Like blog posts, podcast episodes usually have a common subject or structure and are distributed once a day, once a week, or according to whatever schedule the podcaster selects.

A podcast can be any sort of audio recording, but there are several common podcast formats. Many podcasts are hosted by a single person who relays news or current events or shares their opinion, observations, or expertise on a given topic, much like a traditional radio show. A podcast can also feature multiple hosts or speakers who chat with each other about selected topics or issues. This format can be a scripted or unscripted conversation or a roundtable discussion among several people. For example, KQED's "Forum" podcast (*www.kqed.org/radio/programs/forum*) starts as a live radio show where pundits or experts on particular topics call in to participate in a recorded discussion. The recording is made available online as a podcast and can be downloaded from the KQED website. Podcasts can also be a series of interviews, where one or more hosts talks to a guest or guests. CBS News' "60 Minutes" podcast (*www.cbsnews.com/podcasts*) usually includes reports on various news stories relayed by journalists around the world and includes interviews with newsmakers and key players.

For examples of journalism and news podcasts
go to **djhandbook.net/newspodcasts**

Podcasts aren't limited to just audio either. Video podcasts, or *vodcasts,* include both video and audio. Podcast producers can also create "enhanced" podcasts that function like a slideshow and include breaks or markers that allow listeners to skip ahead to various points in the podcast. An enhanced podcast can include images or web addresses that appear at predetermined points in the podcast when the file is played on a computer or a compatible audio player.

There is no set formula for what a podcast should include or how it should be structured, but there are some common elements found in many podcasts. Each podcast episode often begins with an announcement of the title of the podcast or episode, as well as an introduction of the host and/or topic. Some podcasts also include an introduction of the speakers or guests and a brief summary of what will be covered in the episode. Some podcasts also have their own theme music that is played at the beginning or the end of the recording. For example, ABC News (*abcnews.go.com/Technology/Podcasting*) includes the first few notes of its signature theme at the beginning of many of its podcasts. Podcasts are often ended with an announcement of the name of the podcast and a verbal appreciation to the listener for tuning in. Most podcasts also announce the web address where listeners can hear or download additional episodes.

Podcasts are great for journalists who, because of the unlimited space the internet provides, are not confined by the time restrictions of broadcast media. The audio sessions included in podcasts can also be much more informal than programs heard on traditional media. Some podcasts are a simple chat where the host talks directly to the audience or are an impromptu discussion on a selected topic. Podcasts aren't limited just to mainstream news organizations or journalists. Many podcasts are created by people unaffiliated with a traditional media outlet who have access to audio recording equipment and want to share their thoughts or knowledge about a particular subject.

Creating a podcast requires just a few audio tools, usually one or more microphones for recording the speaker(s), computer software for recording and editing the audio, and a pair of headphones for monitoring the audio quality. Recording a podcast is like recording any audio file and can be edited to include narration, interviews, soundbites, or any combination of audio elements.

Before you begin your first podcast, you should first select a topic or focus for your series. Each episode should be consistent and have a similar format that the returning listener can expect to hear. Before you record each show, you should first identify what you want to discuss during the podcast and what other audio elements you will include. Podcasts can be unscripted, but shouldn't lack focus or direction. Write notes on the talking points you will mention during the recording and, if you plan to include interviews or a roundtable discussion, prepare a list of possible questions or conversation starters in advance. Planning the podcast before you begin recording lessens the chance that you will digress from the topic or struggle to come up with something to say.

Podcasts can range in length from just a few minutes to over an hour depending on the show, but on average last between ten and 30 minutes. Podcasts are often unscripted and can therefore be lengthy. There are no time restrictions on a podcast, so the length of your recording should depend on the content. Podcasts, especially those produced by professional news media, should be edited before they are posted online to tighten up the conversation, eliminate unnecessary audio elements, and lessen the time required to listen to them. This means eliminating pauses, ums and ahs, and moments where the host or guest digressed from the topic. No matter the length, podcasts should be engaging from beginning to end.

Once you create audio files for your podcast, you should next post them online and make them available through a podcast feed. A podcast is not just a group of audio files posted to the web. True podcasts are audio files that are syndicated using an RSS or *XML* feed. This feed allows the listener to subscribe to the podcast and be notified when new episodes are available. A podcast feed is created by writing a short bit of code into a plain text file, which requires knowledge of computer languages such as HTML or XML, or by using one of tools like iTunes (*www.apple.com/iTunes*) or blogging tools like WordPress or TypePad that do not require technical knowledge from the user.

 For directions on how to create a podcast feed, as well as tutorials and resources go to **djhandbook.net/podcasts**

Once you upload your audio files to the web and create a podcast feed, you can submit the web address of the feed to a podcast aggregator like iTunes, where listeners can preview and subscribe to the series. iTunes (*www.apple.com/ itunes/podcasts*), the popular music management software and online media store, is home to hundreds of thousands of podcasts dedicated to a range of topics and are submitted by a diverse group of contributors.

iTunes

Listeners can use a podcast delivery system like iTunes to download each episode individually or automatically download new episodes when they become available. You can also embed podcasts on a website using an embedded audio player or create links to individual audio files so they can be downloaded directly from the website. Podcast episodes are often listened to long after they are first published, so you should maintain an archive from which your audience can download and listen to older episodes. Let visitors know about your podcast by adding links on your main website to your podcast feed or the location where potential listeners can subscribe.

Like blogging, podcasting requires a significant time commitment, so you should podcast about something you are passionate about and won't grow tired of. Creating podcasts centered on subjects and issues you find interesting will likely attract listeners who are equally interested in the subject. There are hundreds of thousands of podcasts available on the web and it is important to offer a unique format or point of view that makes your podcast stand out from the rest. Podcasts should make the listener want to listen to not only the first episode, but later episodes as well. If you continue to deliver consistently great content, you will over time build a substantial audience of listeners.

AUDIO SLIDESHOWS

CHAPTER SIX

In print publications such as newspapers or magazines, news stories are sometimes accompanied by a single photo that illustrates the story or, if there is a space, a photo spread in which a group of photographs are printed adjacent to each other. However, sometimes the whole news story can't be told by a single photo or even a few photos. An *audio slideshow* enhances traditional news photography by combining many different photos with sound such as interviews or ambient sound to tell a complete story. In an audio slideshow, photos are displayed one after the other as the audio plays, allowing the viewer to absorb both media at the same time. Audio adds another dimension to photos and can include the voices and sounds of the people, places, and things featured in the slideshow. A print story about a crime victim, for example, relies on the reporter to describe the victim's emotional state. A photo slideshow allows the audience to hear the victim's voice and see the emotion on his or her face, which can draw the viewer further into the story.

Audio slideshows are similar to video in that the viewer can play, pause, rewind, and fast forward a succession of images and audio. Unlike video, the photos included in a slideshow focus on a specific moment instead of action or motion. Audio slideshows are also relatively easier and less-time consuming to produce than video, which makes them especially useful for documenting breaking news stories. For example, after natural disasters such as earthquakes or fires, it is not uncommon for news media to create simple, but captivating audio slideshows using photos shot by a staff photographer and recorded shot by the photographer or other staff journalist.

 For examples of audio slideshows created by online news sites, go to **djhandbook.net/news-slideshows**

Many online slideshows share common features. Photos dominate the majority of the physical space of a slideshow and are the focal point for the viewer. Captions or text that describe each photo usually appear either below the photos or on a transparent layer above the images. Most audio slideshows also include a *scrubber* or other navigation that indicates the progression and total length of the slideshow and can be dragged back and forth to various points in the presentation. Audio slideshows can also include a button that allows the viewer to raise or lower the volume of the audio or turn it off completely.

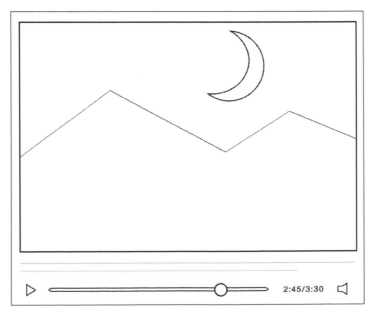

The layout of a typical audio slideshow

A slideshow doesn't always have to include sound. A photo slideshow, a series of images displayed in sequence without accompanying audio, can either be played automatically like a video or let the viewer select the images they want to view. MSNBC's "Week in Pictures" (*www.msnbc.msn.com/id/3842331*), a series of photo slideshows that contain memorable images from the week, incorporates both techniques. The viewer can let the images play in sequence or navigate around the slideshow by clicking links that correspond to each photo. Links included in slideshows can be a series of numbers, photo thumbnails, or arrows, and are often used in place of a scrubber.

Even for slideshows where audio is an essential element of the story, the viewer should be given the option to watch the slideshow without audio. Some online viewers access the web from locations where they cannot or do not want to listen to sound. This should not be a barrier to their ability to watch the slideshow.

Journalists from all forms of media are creating audio slideshows. Some photographers are required to gather audio in addition to shooting photos and print reporters are telling their stories using visual media, as well as writing text stories. Creating an audio slideshow from start to finish requires knowledge of how to properly shoot photos, how to gather and edit audio, and how to tell stories using multiple media. Producing audio slideshows is a great way to learn each of these skills and is great practice for beginning digital journalists.

Creating an audio slideshow in the field requires the producer to both record audio and shoot photos at the same time. There is no set rule of how to gather both media in a single session, but it is almost physically impossible to handle both a camera and an audio recorder at the same time. Ideally, you should shoot photos when something visually interesting happens and pick up the audio recorder to gather interesting ambient sound or to conduct interviews. Effectively managing both tasks, however, only comes with real-world practice. Juggling both media relies on the journalist's instinct to quickly decide what will make for a great photo and what will make for great audio. Before you arrive at an assignment, consider what will happen at the scene and create a plan for what elements you will capture in various media. As you shoot photos and record audio, visualize how what you have documented can later be shaped into a slideshow. Reporters can also split the responsibility with a colleague so that one person captures audio and the other captures photos. If more than one person gathers elements for a single slideshow, everyone involved should form a plan before heading out into the field so that the different media will complement each other once they are assembled.

The audio you record should reflect and contribute to the impact of the photos that you shoot. For example, if you are creating an audio slideshow about a local park, you could record ambient sound of children playing, interviews with park visitors, and other audio elements, as well as shoot photos of these subjects. If the focus of your audio slideshow is a person or people, you should also record their voices either as ambient sound or in a formal interview. Just as photos of people can draw the eye of a reader, hearing voices of people can create a greater connection between the audience and the audio story.

Audio slideshows also require the photographer to gather as many options as possible to pair with the audio. Slideshows often display more than one photo of a single subject or different photos from a single session to illustrate the audio story. Photographers should shoot everything in the scene, including details, various perspectives, and — for human subjects — emotions that will bring the audio to life. You should shoot as many photos as possible, but also remember that each photo must be able to stand on its own. Slideshow viewers will often stare at a single photo for a long time, so each photo should be visually compelling and tell its own story. Blurry, out of focus, or just plain bad photos should not be included in a photo slideshow.

In addition to shooting photos or recording audio, it is also important to write down information about each photo, including the names of the subjects, the location or address of the scene, and descriptive information that can later be included in captions. This information is necessary for slideshows in which captions help the viewer understand what is happening in each photo. Captions should also provide additional information beyond what the viewer can see in the photo such as why the subject was photographed or the background of the story.

Creating the slideshow

After you gather your photos and audio, you should next determine how the combined elements will communicate the story. There are two approaches to creating a narrative for a slideshow. The first is to assemble several photos that together tell a collective story. This type of slideshow has central characters, a story arc, and a beginning, middle, and end. For example, for its slideshow "Criminal Codes" (*seattletimes.nwsource.com/audio/news/local/criminalcodes*), an exploration of a drug treatment program at a local correctional facility, *The Seattle Times* created a slideshow that uses audio and photos to tell the story of an inmate going through the program. The slideshow begins with photos of the facility and ambient sound of correctional officers and inmates. The slideshow continues with an audio interview of a single inmate speaking about how the program has affected him while various photos of the inmate are shown. The slideshow concludes with lively photos and audio of several other inmates and makes the inferred conclusion that the program is helping its participants. This type of audio slideshow is like a short movie that identifies the main characters, sets the story, and concludes with a summary or resolution, all within the span of a few minutes. It is up to the reporter or producer to first identify the narrative and select the photos and audio with the most impact that together tell a story.

The second type of slideshow focuses on a topic or issue, but instead of telling a story, the photos are used to illustrate what is said in the audio. For example, for the slideshow "The Water Dance" (*bit.ly/WaterDance*), *New York Times* photographer Bill Cunningham observes and discusses the humor of pedestrians who try to navigate New York City's deceptively deep rain puddles. As Cunningham speaks, photos of various people dodging the huge puddles are shown. The photos together have no actual narrative, but provide visual examples that underscore the narration.

Although photos and sound used in an audio slideshow rely on each other to tell a complete story, it is the audio that is the foundation of the slideshow. Before selecting the photos that will be included in the presentation, you must first arrange and assemble your audio clips into one audio file. The length of the audio determines the length of the slideshow, the number of photos that can be included the slideshow, and roughly how long each photo is shown.

Most audio slideshows are between two and four minutes long. Any longer risks losing the viewer's attention. Each photograph should appear onscreen for at least three, but no longer than ten seconds — long enough for the viewer to digest the photo, but not so long that the viewer becomes bored and clicks away. The *pacing* or duration of each slide, however, should be dictated by the story. A somber story means the pacing of the slideshow should be slower and have more time between each photo. A slideshow about an upbeat topic should have a faster pace and each photo should be shown for a shorter length of time.

When you edit audio, you should first have an idea of how many photos you have to work with. Too many photos crammed into one slideshow means each photo only appears for a second or two, barely enough time for the viewer to digest each one. Too few photos means each photo remains onscreen too long, making the slideshow feel drawn out and boring. For example, if you only have ten usable photos to include in your slideshow, then a three-minute audio clip will be too long. Edit your audio with the number of photos you'd like to include in mind, but be flexible enough to adjust your story if necessary.

Editing audio can easily become the most time-consuming part of creating an audio slideshow. The audio guides the viewer through the story and directs the narrative and, as such, should be carefully edited with this in mind. Select the audio clips that best tell the story and eliminate any repetitive or unnecessary information. Narration can fill in the gaps when interviews or soundbites aren't available or don't adequately summarize the story. It is okay to add narration to a slideshow, but ideally the story should tell itself without any commentary from the reporter. Once you've edited your audio, you can then select the photos that will shape the rest of the slideshow.

A title card

Instead of a photo, many audio slideshows begin with a *title card*, a graphic at the beginning of the slideshow that displays the name or subject of the slideshow, the name of the photographer(s) or reporter, and optionally an image that represents the content of the presentation. Title cards can be created with a computer graphics program like Photoshop and should also include the name or logo of the news organization. The next image that follows the title card should be the first photograph in the slideshow.

The first photo of the slideshow should establish the scene and draw the viewer into the story. If the slideshow is focused on a specific person, location, or event, the first photo should be of the subject. The last photo in the slideshow should be as strong as the first and leave the viewer with a lasting impression or summarize what the viewer has seen. The beginning and end of a slideshow is what the audience remembers most. The photos in between don't have to be as captivating as the first or the last, but should be compelling enough to hold the viewer's interest.

Photos should be arranged so they match what is discussed in the audio. For example, if the slideshow includes ambient sound of children playing in a park, the photos that appear at that point should show children playing in a park. If the audio in your slideshow includes an interview or soundbite, you should display a photo of the speaker when they begin talking so the viewer can visually identify him or her. The photos that follow should either match what the person is saying or reflect the emotional state of the speaker. If an interviewee describes a sad time in his or her life, you shouldn't show a photo of them looking cheery. If they are talking about a great party they attended, show photos from the party, if they are available. Photos should complement the audio, not compete with it.

There is no magic formula for creating a great slideshow, but the best are those that keep the viewer engaged from start to finish. The slideshow producer should use the best audio and photos possible to draw the audience into the story. The viewer can stop the slideshow at any time — your goal is to make them want to watch the presentation from start to finish.

Soundslides

Soundslides (*www.soundslides.com*), a computer program used to create Flash-based slideshows, does not require knowledge of Flash to use and is a popular tool in many newsrooms. The software was developed by photographer/ multimedia producer Joe Weiss as a way for journalists to create slideshows using a very simple and intuitive interface. Using Soundslides, anyone can create a slideshow in as little as five minutes. The software is available for both Macs and PCs for a nominal fee. Soundslides Plus, which has advanced features like the ability to include subtitles, animate photos, create slideshows without audio, and export slideshows as video, is available for a slightly higher price.

Soundslides

There are just a few steps to creating an audio slideshow in Soundslides. Before you create your slideshow, your photos should be assembled and placed in a single folder on your computer. Your audio should be edited and ready to be imported into the program. You cannot edit either media in Soundslides. Your audio can be any length, but must be saved as an MP3 file. Your photos can be any shape or size, but must be saved as JPG files. If there is a problem with the audio or any of the photos, the elements can be edited outside of Soundslides and new versions can be imported to replace the original files.

Once you import the photos and audio into Soundslides, the photos are distributed evenly on a timeline. The length of the timeline is equal to the length of your audio file. Soundslides can also create slideshows without audio that are set at a predetermined length. You can assemble and arrange the photos in any order along the timeline as you would in a basic audio or video editing program. You can also adjust the length of time each image appears in the slideshow. Photos should stop and start at natural pauses or breaks in the audio like when a person begins or is finished speaking, which lessens the chance for awkward or distracting transitions.

Soundslides also includes a space to create captions for each image and add headlines and credits that are displayed adjacent to the photos. When a photo is taken with a digital camera, *metadata* or information about the photo such as the date and time it was taken or the model of the camera is stored along with the image in a digital file. Using a photo editing program like Photoshop, photographers can add additional information to the metadata such as credits or captions. Soundslides can pull the information saved in the metadata and include it as a caption in the slideshow. Slideshow producers can also alter the slideshow template to change the appearance of the final presentation and include or exclude various features.

Once the slideshow is finished, Soundslides creates a folder that contains the files needed to display the slideshow online. This includes Flash files as well as the HTML files necessary to display these Flash files, all of which are made available in a single folder that can be uploaded to the web. The entire created folder should be uploaded to the site where the slideshow will be viewed. You can then create a link to the final slideshow or embed it in any compatible web page.

For Soundslides tutorials and alternatives to the program go to **djhandbook.net/soundslides**

There are several other ways to create photo slideshows. Some producers use video editing programs like Final Cut to build audio slideshows. Creating a slideshow in an advanced editing program allows the producer to integrate video as well as photos and audio into a single video package. Audio slideshows saved as video files also give the producer greater flexibility over where the slideshow can be posted. Video slideshows can be uploaded to video sharing sites like YouTube (*www.youtube.com*) or embedded in a web page using an embeddable video player. You can also use Flash, outlined in Chapter 11, to create slideshows instead of using Soundslides. Flash slideshows can be customized down to the tiniest detail, but unlike Soundslides, the program requires technical knowledge of design and computer programming to use.

VIDEO

CHAPTER SEVEN

Photos are great for capturing a single moment in time and audio is great for documenting voices and sounds. Video is a like a combination of the two media and can also capture action and motion. Visual stories like a high-speed car chase or an action-packed football game can be told using other media, but video brings these stories to life using moving images.

There are many ways online video is used in journalism. Video can be as simple as an interview with a newsmaker or footage of a news event. Television stations use the web to make video reports and newscasts available online after they are broadcast. Documentary filmmakers post feature-length video to the web and making clips of longer pieces available to an online audience. Video can also be combined with blogging to create a *video blog* or *vlog*, a series of video entries in which a person shares their thoughts or opinions or regularly posts interesting video clips. Video can also be combined with other media such as text, photos, and audio to create multimedia and interactive stories.

The web can also be used as a platform to broadcast live television as it happens. Live webcasts have become increasingly popular, especially during major news events when they are viewed by millions of web users. For example, after the 2009 death of pop singer Michael Jackson, several news stations streamed the memorial service live on the web. Online audiences can also watch regular television broadcasts on the web, 24 hours a day. Television channels like CNN (*www.cnn.com/live*) and C-SPAN (*www.c-span.org/Watch/C-SPAN.aspx*) offer viewers the option of watching live broadcasts on either their television, computer, or both.

For examples of online video journalism
go to **djhandbook.net/videojournalism**

As internet connection speeds get faster and the quality of online video improves, many more internet users are watching video on the web. YouTube (*www.youtube.com*), the online video sharing site where users can upload, view, and share videos, is visited daily by millions of web users and ushered in a new era of online video. Because of sites like YouTube, online audiences are more likely to sit in front of their computers for extended periods of time to watch online video. Sites like Hulu (*www.hulu.com*), which hosts full-length movies and television shows, encourage web users to watch video for hours at a time. Newsrooms have capitalized on this trend by producing high-quality online video that caters to web audiences.

The cost of video production, including cameras, accessories, and video editing software has decreased dramatically — so much so that high-quality video doesn't have to be created by professional journalists. Much of the video posted online is created by ordinary citizens armed with video equipment. Online video can be created with just a video camera and a computer with video editing software. Journalists and videographers often use higher quality video cameras, microphones, headphones, and tripods to create the best video quality possible. Video produced with inexpensive equipment won't automatically deter potential viewers, but online audiences expect quality video from professional media organizations and will not accept poor video, with some exceptions.

Video can be time-consuming to both record and edit, which should be considered before attempting to produce video stories or projects. Video journalism often requires the videographer to record as many details and parts of the scene as possible which then must be edited down to a few minutes before it is posted online. However, video production can be as simple or as complex as you make it. Non-broadcast news outlets and smaller news organizations for whom video is not the primary medium should focus their resources on stories or content will attract a significant audience and draw interest for a considerable time after it is published. This ensures that resources are invested in projects that have a long shelf life.

Shooting video is as easy as clicking the record button on a camera, but well-produced video takes skill, practice, and, most importantly, a visual eye. Online video doesn't have to be slick, but it should be captivating and well-executed.

Choosing a camera

To create video for either the web or for a traditional on-air broadcast, you will need a digital video (DV) camera. DV cameras are smaller and lighter than their clunky predecessors and are great for on-the-go recording and mobile journalism.

Digital video cameras are often categorized by the *resolution* or level of detail of the video. Digital video is made of tiny dots called *pixels*. The higher the resolution of the camera, the more pixels the video contains, which means it can be displayed at larger sizes without appearing blurry or out-of-focus. For example, video shot on a camera with a lower resolution and displayed on a standard television will appear blurry because there are fewer pixels that make up the image. Video resolution is often measured in *megapixels*, a measurement equal to 1 million pixels. High definition or HD cameras have more pixels and a higher resolution which means they can record and display a more detailed image.

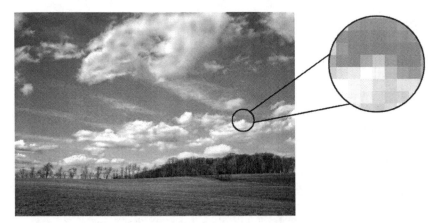

A digital image is made of millions of dots called "pixels"

Digital video cameras range from basic consumer models to more expensive professional models and have a varying assortment of features. Video cameras can be divided into three categories: professional, *point-and-shoot*, a term used to describe cameras that do not require input from the videographer, and *prosumer*, a camera that falls somewhere between the two categories. All three types of cameras share common functions such as record and playback and features such as LCD screens and zoom controls.

Many digital video cameras are equipped with an *LCD screen* that is used to view the video as it is recording and to play back what is recorded. LCD, short for liquid crystal display, can be used instead of the video camera's *viewfinder*, the small window on the camera used to frame the image. To use a viewfinder, the camera operator must place their eye directly on the camera to view the recording. An LCD screen allows the videographer to stand back from the camera and see what the camera is recording. Some cameras include both a viewfinder and an LCD screen to give the videographer flexibility over how they view the recording. LCD screens require a significant amount of power so the video camera should be plugged into an electrical outlet to prevent the LCD screen from draining power from the camera's battery.

Digital video cameras are often equipped with *optical zoom*, which allows the videographer to electronically focus the camera's lens to obtain a closer or farther image without physically moving the camera. When the camera zooms

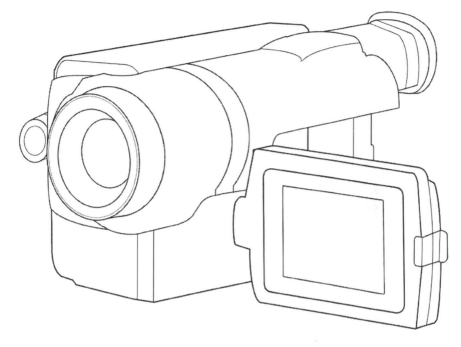

A typical digital video camera

in, the camera electronically adjusts the focus to get a closer image. When the camera is zoomed out, the camera widens the focus to capture more of the scene. The zoom button is usually a rocker or set of buttons on top of the camera, sometimes marked "T" for toward and "W" for withdraw. Usually, the harder you press the rocker or buttons, the quicker the camera will zoom. Some professional video cameras allow the videographer to zoom manually by turning the focus ring located around the camera's lens. Some cameras also have *digital zoom*, an electronic feature that appears to zoom in even closer to the subject than regular optical zoom. Digital zoom doesn't actually zoom further — instead it crops the edges of the digital video to make it appear as if it was closer. Shooting video with digital zoom can cause *pixelation* or blurry or reduced-quality video. For this reason, professional videographers should not use digital zoom.

Many basic point-and-shoot video cameras can automatically control many of the camera's functions such as focus and *exposure,* the amount of light received by the camera's sensor, and can easily be used by someone with little to no video recording experience. Like photo cameras, point-and-shoot video cameras usually offer few or no manual controls and automatically adjust according to light or movement captured by the camera. One such automatic control found on many point-and-shoot video cameras is *autofocus*, which electronically calculates whether the picture is in focus and automatically adjusts the camera so that the video is as clear as possible. Autofocus works well for subjects that don't move, but should be disabled when recording any sort of action. Autofocus refocuses the camera anytime the subject or the camera moves and any sudden motion will cause the camera to lose and attempt to regain focus, resulting in a temporarily blurry picture. If you anticipate your subject will make any quick movements, it is best to turn off the autofocus feature, which on most cameras is found in the camera menu.

The human hand is naturally unsteady when holding a video camera which can create video that looks like it was shot during an earthquake. To combat this problem, some video cameras are also equipped with *image stabilization*, a feature that electronically corrects shaky footage. Image stabilization crops a portion of the video image to reduce the visible shakiness of the video.

Some video cameras are equipped with a small light built into the front of the camera that is used to illuminate the subject. The built-in light can create harsh shadows and should only be used when absolutely necessary. On the other hand, many basic point-and-shoot video cameras produce video that is dark and hard to see if there isn't enough light available to obtain a proper image. Video recorded under low light contains "noise" or a grainy image that is created because the camera's sensor does not have enough information to properly record the video. To eliminate this problem, use available sources of light such as sunlight or lamps to illuminate your subject.

For examples of common video problems and how to correct them, go to **djhandbook.net/badvideo**

High-end, professional cameras differ from point-and-shoot cameras in that the videographer can manually control the camera's settings and the resulting image. Most professional cameras include a feature that allows the videographer to adjust the color or tint of the video. *White balance*, an electronic process that corrects the color captured by the camera, is used to ensure that the colors recorded by the camera's sensor are true to life. For example, video shot outdoors may appear too blue and video shot indoors may look too orange because of an imbalance of the video's *color temperature,* a measurement of the color emitted by various light sources. The white balance feature uses a white object as a reference point, often a blank sheet of paper held up in front of the camera by the operator, and uses that information to accurately represent the rest of the color spectrum. Point-and-shoot video cameras often white balance the image automatically and sometimes incorrectly, which can create odd-colored video.

Some high-end cameras can also shoot still photographs as well as video. However, the ability to capture quality photographs — the kind that can be used in print or online — is a feature more likely included on pricier, professional cameras and not the average inexpensive video camera. If you plan to shoot photos, use a dedicated digital photo camera that can shoot higher-quality photos.

Some point-and-shoot cameras include professional features like manual focus and white balance. There cameras are often called *prosumer* cameras, or video cameras that are both easy to use and have professional features. These cameras are often pricier than basic video cameras, but are less expensive than the high-end cameras used by broadcast journalists.

Nearly all video cameras are equipped with built-in microphones that should not be used when recording professional video. These internal microphones pick up any and all sounds near the camera. The farther the video camera is from the subject, the more background noise the camera will record, which can result in unusable video, especially when recording targeted sounds such as interviews. The audio recorded by a video camera is equally important as the video it records. Whichever camera you select, it should be equipped with headphone and microphone inputs that allow the operator to connect external equipment. Higher-end cameras are often equipped with XLR input jacks for connecting professional microphones and basic cameras are equipped with TRS inputs (see Chapter 5 for a detailed description of these connection systems). These connections make it easier to monitor and record better audio.

In addition to the features they include, digital video cameras also can be classified by the type of media to which they record. DV cameras can record in a range of formats, including MiniDV, DVD, internal hard drives, and memory cards.

MiniDV is a digital video format that is popular among journalists. MiniDV cameras record on a cassette that is about half the size of a standard deck of playing cards and can record 60 to 90 minutes of video, depending on the record mode. The format captures excellent video and sound quality, but the video produced by the camera must be imported in real-time to a computer. This means for every minute of video that you record, you have to wait one minute for the footage to be transferred to the computer.

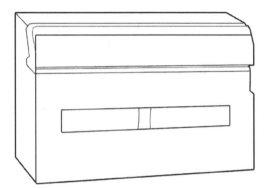

A MiniDV cassette

MiniDV cameras usually require a cable to connect the camera to the computer. There are two common types of cable connection systems: USB and FireWire. USB, short for Universal Serial Bus, is a system for connecting a computer to a video camera or other electronic equipment. USB is standard on modern computers and is also used to connect many other electronic devices. *FireWire* is another connection system used to transfer information between a computer and a camera or other electronic equipment. FireWire can transfer more data at higher speeds than a USB cable and is standard on many video cameras and most newer Mac computers and laptops. Before purchasing a camera with a FireWire connection, verify that your computer has a FireWire input.

Another common type of digital video camera is the hard drive camera which can save video directly to an internal drive, eliminating the need to carry blank tapes or cassettes. The recorded video is transferred directly to the computer using a USB or FireWire connection and does not require the wait time associated with MiniDV cameras. However, hard drive cameras can only record as much video as the drive can store.

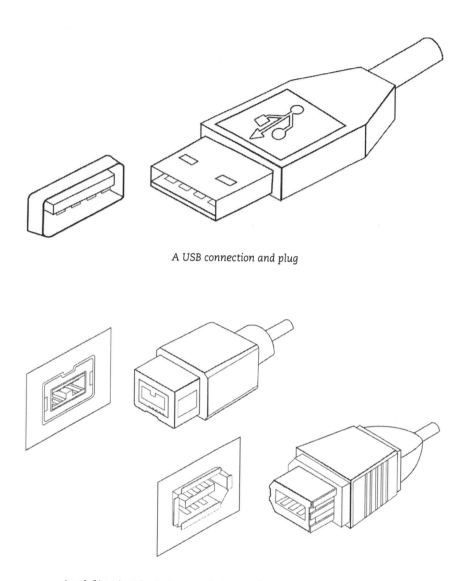

A USB connection and plug

(top left)A FireWire 800 port and plug; a FireWire 400 port and plug, two
common FireWire connections

Some digital video cameras, including those with internal drives, also use
memory cards to store video. Memory cards are removable storage devices, usually
about the size of a postage stamp, that can hold varying amounts of video or
other digital media depending on the capacity of the card. Memory cards are
also used for photo cameras and the format makes it easy to transfer video to
a computer using a USB or FireWire connection. Video recorded on memory

cards can also be transferred to a computer using a *memory card reader*, an external drive that is connected to the computer using a USB or FireWire connection. A card reader allows the videographer to remove the memory card from the camera and insert it into the card reader. Once the card is inserted in the reader, a folder appears on the computer that contains the video files.

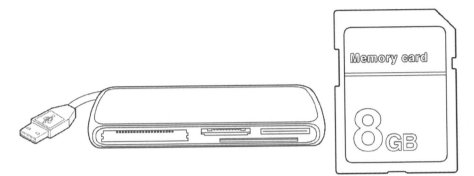

A memory card reader (left) and memory card (enlarged to show detail)

A less popular option among digital journalists is the DVD camera which, instead of cassettes or internal drives, records video to compact DVDs. MiniDVDs are about half the size of regular DVD discs and can be played in a DVD player or computer that has a tray for inserting discs. MiniDVD cameras can record 20 to 60 minutes of footage on each DVD, depending on the record mode. However, because DVD cameras record video directly to discs, the format is not useful for any video that needs to be edited, which, in journalism, is pretty much all video.

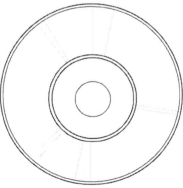

A MiniDVD disc (not actual size)

Video doesn't have to be shot on a dedicated video camera for it to be useful for journalism. Some people, especially those who happen to be in the right place at the right time, use cell phones that can record video to capture the news. Many more people own cell phone cameras than digital video cameras and because people are more likely to carry a cell phone with them, they can quickly record news events as they unfold. For example, video of the 2007 Virginia Tech shooting that left 32 dead and 23 wounded was captured on a cell phone by a student of the university. The cell phone video was eventually posted to YouTube and aired on major news networks where it was collectively viewed by millions of people. At the time, some questioned whether the amateur video was actually journalism, but despite how it was recorded and who recorded it, the video undoubtedly provided an unmatched look inside the tragic event. Although video recorded with cell phone cameras is dramatically improving with each new generation of phones, professional journalists should use dedicated video cameras whenever possible. Digital video cameras can store higher quality video and more of it.

When selecting a video camera, consider your budget, where the video will appear, and the features necessary to record the quality of video you require. A less expensive camera can produce video that looks great on a computer screen, while a broadcast-quality camera produces higher quality video, but also has a higher price. The type of camera you select should also depend on the skill level of the videographer. An expensive digital video camera won't instantly transform you into a professional videographer. Novice videographers can experiment with less expensive models before moving on to higher-end cameras with more complex features. Read the manual included with the video camera and become familiar with its features and capabilities before you begin shooting. Once you become familiar with the camera, you will spend less time adjusting or setting up your shots and more quickly shooting and recording excellent video.

Camera accessories

To capture great video you need more than just a great camera. Aside from the video camera, the most important tool in video production is the *tripod*, three telescoping rods with a mount on top that steadies and supports the camera and prevents the shaky video a handheld camera can produce. A tripod also helps to maintain a balanced horizon so the video doesn't appear tilted or askew. A good tripod should be light enough to carry around, but also strong enough to keep the camera from tipping over, especially in strong winds. Many tripods also come with a leveling bubble that indicates if the camera is perfectly in position. Alternatively, videographers can also use a monopod, which has one leg instead of three. A tripod is sometimes used for still photography, but is not essential for shooting a steady image. The opposite is true for video which captures motion, often for an extended period of time.

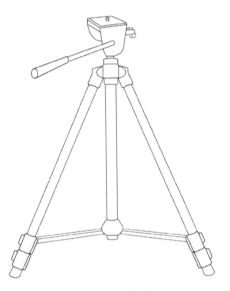

A typical tripod

Another essential tool for professional video recording are microphones, which are outlined in Chapter 5. Microphones are essential for interviews where recording the subject's voice as clearly as possible is especially important. Along with a tripod and microphone, video journalists also need a quality pair of headphones to monitor the audio recorded by the camera. Other essential accessories include a power cord for charging the camera, extra tapes and batteries, lens cleaner or wipes, an extension cord for plugging the camera into distant electric outlets, and a camera bag to carry it all in. Videographers often can carry a lot of equipment and a camera bag helps keep everything easily accessible.

For a guide to commonly used video cameras and accessories, go to **djhandbook.net/videocameras**

Composing video

Anyone can pick up a video camera and start shooting. What separates professional videographers from amateurs is an attention to composition and a conscious effort to produce aesthetically pleasing video. The first step to creating visually appealing video is knowing how to frame the image. There are several common *shots*, or ways to frame video, including wide shots, medium shots, and close-ups, that are used in specific ways to tell a story or communicate more about the subject.

To create a *wide shot*, also called a *long shot*, the camera is positioned at a distance from the subject to capture a large area of the scene. Wide shots are also called *establishing shots* because the framing technique is used to establish the scene and informs the viewer about the location of the story. For example, a wide shot for a video story about a skier could include the snow, the trees, and the mountains in the frame to show the skier's environment. Wide shots are often used in television journalism to communicate a story, but do not work as well on the web because of a computer's comparatively small screen size. The details that a viewer can see on a larger television screen cannot be viewed as easily on the average computer.

In a *close-up* shot, the video is framed very close to the subject to reveal details like a single flower in a garden or the face of an interviewee. Because of the intimate proximity of the camera, close-up shots are frequently used in interviews to show reactions or emotions and make the viewer feel more connected to the subject. A close-up of a person in which only the head and shoulders are visible in the frame is called a *talking head* because the rest of the body is out of frame. Close-ups work well on the web and small computer screens.

Every shot that isn't a wide shot or close up is likely a *medium shot*, though there is no measurable boundary that separates one shot from another. A medium shot usually frames a person from the waist up and is used to show the subject's body language and include some of the surrounding environment.

Most camera shots can be classified as wide, medium, or close-ups, though there are many variations and in-between shots such as the *extreme close-up* or the *medium long shot*.

(from top) A wide shot; a medium shot; a close-up

In addition to proper framing, there are a few guidelines to follow to make your video appear more professional. Many of these guidelines are the same as the principles of photography outlined in Chapter 4. Video composition borrows heavily from still photography techniques except that video usually captures subjects that are in motion.

Videographers, like photographers, should follow the *rule of thirds* which dictates that when composing an image, the videographer should mentally divide the image into thirds, both vertically and horizontally, similar to a tic-tac-toe board. Instead of placing the subject of the video in the exact center of the frame, move the subject slightly off-center at one of the four intersecting points on the imaginary grid. Unlike still photography, the videographer must decide whether to maintain the rule of thirds for moving subjects or to disregard the rule and let the subject move about the frame. The rule of thirds is more commonly used in video interviews where the subject is positioned two-thirds of the way from the left edge of the frame.

Well-framed shots should include *head room* or space between the top of the subject's head and the top of the frame. There should be just enough space so that the subject's head is not at the very top of the frame, but not so much that the extra space overtakes the shot.

The image on the left does not include head room; the image on the right includes head room

Video should also be framed to include *nose room* or space between the subject and the direction in which he or she is looking. Also called *lead room*, this framing technique gives the impression that the person is looking at or talking to someone just off-screen. Lead room also indicates the direction in which action is headed. For example, if an athlete is running across a field, lead room should be included on the side of the screen that corresponds with the direction that the athlete is running.

The image on the left does not include nose room; the image on the right includes nose room

When shooting video, avoid visual distractions that take the viewer's eyes off the subject such as an overpowering background or other visual elements. Like photos, this can include distracting elements such as trees and phone poles that appear to grow out of the subject's head. In video, this can also include a person waving in the background, a gathering crowd of onlookers, or passing vehicle traffic.

In addition to common framing techniques, videographers also use key camera movements to capture video and motion. One of the most commonly used camera movements is *zoom* or electronically adjusting the camera's lens to obtain a closer or farther image without physically moving the camera. When the camera zooms in, the camera adjusts the focus to get a closer image. When the camera is zoomed out, the camera widens the focus to take in more of the scene.

To *pan* is to move the camera left or right on a horizontal axis to show the scene or to follow a subject. For example, if a person is walking down a street, you can pan the camera to keep the person in frame. Panning should be done smoothly and at a consistent speed to ensure a great shot.

To tilt is to move the camera up or down on a vertical axis. The motion created by tilting the camera is similar to someone nodding their head "yes". Tilting the camera is similar to panning, but instead of moving side to side, the camera moves up and down.

Zooming, panning, and tilting can be done without a tripod, but doing so can make shots look jerky and unsteady. A tripod also ensures that video is shot at eye-level. The camera should be set on top of a tripod and raised or lowered so the camera is at the same level as the subject's eyes without tilting the camera up or down. Tilting the camera at an angle to frame the subject creates *ascending* or *descending* shots, which makes a person look like either a giant or a dwarf, respectively.

 To see examples of these camera movements
go to **djhandbook.net/cameramoves**

Video shot by a novice videographer is easy to spot — it is usually shaky, dark, grainy, askew, or any combination of these. Following these guidelines and framing techniques will help eliminate some of these problems and make your video appear more professional.

Recording in the field

When news breaks, a videographer must grab a camera and head to the scene, often with little preparation and a vague idea of what needs to be filmed. For those video projects for which prep time is available, it is a good idea to *storyboard* or brainstorm what the video piece should look like before you go out and shoot. A storyboard can be a list of shots that you want to include in your video piece or rough sketches that outline and visualize the shots you want to record, including variations such as wide, medium, or close-up shots. Take a minute to write notes or sketch the various setups, interviews, and shots you'd like to capture on location. For example, for a story about a restaurant, you may want to include interviews with the chefs, shots of the food, video of people eating, etc. Drawing a storyboard is useful for planning what you will shoot, but your plan should also be flexible and open to spontaneous or unexpected moments or action. The story itself shouldn't be planned ahead, but at least by brainstorming, you'll have an idea of what you'll want to shoot.

For novice videographers, a good chunk of the time spent in the field is dedicated to setting up and adjusting the video camera's various settings. Before

A storyboard

heading out for a shoot, become familiar with the camera and aware of how to quickly access essential features like white balance and focus. Whenever possible, show up to the scene early and survey the field to get an idea of what you will record. Check your camera's settings before each setup and make sure the video is in focus and that the image is white-balanced. If you use a tripod, make sure the tripod is steady and the picture is balanced. If you don't have a tripod, you must still find a way to capture steady, usable video. You can try placing the camera on a stack of books or leaning against a wall while holding the camera to keep the camera from shaking.

Video is only as good as its audio, so before each shot, test your audio levels and make sure the audio is recording properly. Audio meters can indicate if the device is recording the sound, but use headphones to be sure and, if possible, keep them on for the duration of the shoot.

Video shot indoors can be dark and appear grainy if there isn't enough light to properly record the image. To counteract poor lighting, open window shades or curtains and turn on lamps, overhead lights, or anything that will fill the room with light. Videographers can also use light kits, a set of portable, professional lamps and accessories, but these lamps are often bulky and take time to set up. Light kits are also not as handy for capturing action or motion because the subject may step out of the lighting setup.

Shooting outdoors helps solve many lighting problems. The sun's natural light makes video appear clear and even. When shooting outdoors, position the camera so the sun is behind you and shining directly on the subject. Doing the reverse can cause the camera to focus on the light behind the subject and creates backlighting, a halo effect that makes the subject appear dark and obscured, a problem especially common among point-and-shoot video cameras. Also, avoid shooting in the middle of the day when the sun is directly overhead. When the sun shines down on a person, it casts shadows on the face that obscure the person's eyes and makes them appear menacing. Shooting on a cloudy day or in a shadowy area can diffuse harsh sunlight and create even lighting for your video.

Before you press the record button on the camera, look at your shot and make sure it is properly framed. For each shot you record, you should first shoot preroll, a few seconds of video before each shot, and postroll, a few seconds after the shot. Most video editing programs require a short amount of footage before and after a video clip to create transitions such as fades and dissolves between clips. Video clips that immediately begin with the action can be difficult to edit or apply special effects to. Recording preroll and postroll in the field allow you to create proper transitions when you later edit your video.

Most video stories include an establishing shot, a wide shot that captures the scene and identifies the location of the story. Look for identifying landmarks that will give the viewer an idea of where the action is taking place. The rest of the shots you capture are totally up to you. Try to shoot what you think will best communicate the story you intend to tell. Look for action and emotions and situations where people are doing something instead of describing it. Aim to capture each shot in a variety of angles such as wide, medium, and close-up to give yourself options in the editing room. Also, you don't have to shoot your video in the sequence that it will appear in the final piece. When you edit your video, you can assemble what you've shot into any order you choose.

Be sure to record each shot for at least ten seconds so it is usable and is long enough for the viewer to understand what is happening. In videography, there is nothing worse than having a great shot that is useless because it is too short. On the other hand, beware of shooting too much video. An itchy trigger finger will create lots of extra video that must be watched and edited, which means you will more time editing your project. Before you hit the record button, ask yourself if the shot is necessary to tell the story.

Shooting nothing but interviews and talking heads will result in boring video. In addition to your main shots, you should also shoot b-roll, supplemental video footage that supports or illustrates the main story. B-roll can refer to any video that is not an interview or a stand-up (video of the reporter talking directly to the camera) and is intercut with the main shots in a news package or video clip. For example, a video interview of a teacher can be intercut with b-roll of the classroom, children working, the teacher writing on the chalkboard, etc. B-roll is used to illustrate what the speaker is describing and to make long interviews less dull. You should keep a log of what b-roll you shoot so you can refer to it once you begin editing. You can also note whether a shot was good or bad and whether it should be included in the final piece.

News can happen at any moment so as a videographer, you must be ready to move quickly and start recording at any time. For events like speeches and meetings, the opposite is true — you'll have to stay still or be very quiet for long periods of time. If you find yourself shooting for a while, avoid fidgeting with the camera or adjusting settings while recording static shots like interviews, which can be distracting to the viewer and cause mismatched edits. Instead, frame the interviewee or shot at the beginning of the recording session and do not adjust the camera again until the person is finished or if they move out of frame.

Shoot and record as discretely as possible, especially when documenting breaking news. The presence of a video camera can influence how people behave in front of it, so be aware of situations where people are putting on an act for the camera. If you sense that a subject's behavior has changed in the presence of the camera, consider moving on to another shot. A video journalist should try to reflect reality in the same way that a reporter or a still photographer does. Never ask someone to recreate what they were just doing or to do something they were not doing before. This is equal to making up a quote in print and violates the principles of journalism.

As a video journalist, you'll have a lot to juggle: recording the video, monitoring video and audio levels, and sometimes engaging the subject in a conversation or interview. Even with all these responsibilities, remember to look up from the camera to observe what is happening around you. There may sometimes be other action happening nearby that you'll also want to record.

Shoot the best video you can while in the field so you'll have as many options as possible once you begin editing. Pay special attention to how the video is framed and whether each shot communicates a part of the story to the audience.

Interviewing

News video often includes interviews where the reporter asks one or more people questions about a topic or issue. Video interviews are great for recording eyewitness reports, reactions to news events, or to gain a deeper insight into the speaker. Compelling video interviews are anchored by strong characters and personalities who can vividly describe a scene or their feelings or emotions. This may not, however, be everyone you interview. Some people are camera-shy and reluctant to be interviewed with a video camera and a microphone in their face. If the situation allows, look for interviewees who are comfortable expressing themselves on camera and do not be afraid to move on to the next person if they cannot do so.

If you have time, talk to the interviewee for a minute before you set up the camera, which can make them feel more relaxed. A pre-interview chat can also help you understand how the subject moves and how you should frame your shot. Some people, for example, gesture when they talk so you may have to zoom the camera out to include the gestures in the frame. Others may have more expressive faces which means the camera can be framed close to better capture the emotion.

Interviews should be framed according to the rule of thirds with the head and upper chest visible in the frame. The subject should be shot from a slight angle instead of facing the camera directly, which creates a sense of depth. Stand on one side of the camera and ask the interviewee to look directly at you, not at the camera.

A video interview setup

Before the interview begins, have the subject speak naturally into the microphone for as long as it takes to determine that the audio quality is as perfect as possible and that he or she is being properly recorded. If you are both recording and interviewing, you should keep your headphones on, but remain engaged with the interviewee. Alternatively, you can keep both headphones on, but slide the arc of the headphones to the nape of you neck or listen with just one headphone so the person knows you are listening to him or her.

Whenever possible, shoot several interviews to get a variety of opinions or perspectives that you can include in your story. After you shoot an interview, also shoot b-roll of the things the person talked about and the surrounding environment so the footage can also be included in the final video piece.

Video editing

Before a video is broadcast or posted online it is usually edited for length or to assemble video clips into a single narrative or story. Editing video is like putting together the pieces of a puzzle without knowing what the final image will look like. It is up to the editor to visualize the final video project and the clips that will help shape it.

The first step in video editing is to first decide on a storyline. Like a good movie, video storytelling should have a strong beginning and end and an engaging narrative to connect the two. Think about your favorite movie and what made that movie good. Chances are the film had an enjoyable or interesting story. The same narrative structure on which many great movies are based can also be applied to video journalism.

Most Hollywood movies consist of three acts. The first act builds up the story or background and highlights the central issue or characters. The second act introduces the obstacle that the character(s) must overcome. The third act is the climax or resolution where the story comes to an end. The same story arc can be applied to online and broadcast video. Instead of two hours, you have just a few minutes to develop your three acts. Most video stories that appear online are at the most four to five minutes long to ensure that the video is watched from beginning to end by online viewers. Good video, no matter how long or how short, must have strong central characters, as well as a conflict and a resolution. Following the three act structure, a story about a robbery could start with an explanation of how the robbery happened (the first act), a discussion of how the crime affects the neighborhood (second act), and what police and members of the community are doing about it (third act). Once you have outlined how your story will be structured, you can begin editing and assembling your clips.

Video editing is a time-consuming process that can take much longer than shooting. The rise of digital technology, however, has significantly decreased the time necessary to edit video. In the past, video clips were copied in sequence from one tape to another in a process called *linear editing*. The editor had to start at the beginning of the video and copy clips to another tape until the video was complete. This was a painstaking process that allowed little room for mistakes. Digital video is edited using *non-linear editing* systems that allow the editor to alter and arrange any part of the video at any time and in any sequence. The process is similar to using the cut and paste feature in a word processing program to write and arrange text, but instead of words, a video editor can cut, paste, add, delete, or move video or audio clips to construct the final video.

There are various systems and software used for editing digital video. Some of the most popular among journalists are Final Cut, Avid Media Composer, and iMovie. iMovie, a program included on modern Mac computers, and Windows Movie Maker, its PC counterpart, are useful tools for novice video editors or those who don't require extra features to edit their video. Programs like Final Cut and Avid include advanced features and are geared toward professional video editors.

iMovie

iMovie (*www.apple.com/ilife/imovie*) is available as part of the iLife bundle of media tools included with newer Mac computers, along with the audio editor GarageBand and photo editor iPhoto. iMovie has a "drag-and-drop" interface that allows the editor to drag video and audio clips and drop them in the order they should appear in the final clip. Users can import video from a camera directly to iMovie using a FireWire or USB connection or by importing video files from the computer. After uploading video into the program, the user can edit video clips and add titles and music. iMovie also includes basic color correction and video enhancement tools and can create transitions and effects. Recent iteration of the iMovie have additional features such as image stabilization and various advanced video effects. The results of a video edited with iMovie are often comparable to video edited with a professional video editing program.

Windows Movie Maker (*download.live.com/moviemaker*) is free video editing software that is bundled with recent versions of Windows, just as iMovie is included with newer Mac computers. Both programs allow the editor to easily organize and edit video clips using the drag-and-drop method and add audio tracks, titles, and credits. Movie Maker can import video from most video cameras using a FireWire or USB connection. Movie Maker is only for PCs and iMovie is for Macs, but there are other differences that set them apart. Movie Maker has a very different layout and can only import and export certain types of video files while iMovie can save video files in a range of formats.

Windows Movie Maker

Intermediate or experienced video editors more often favor Final Cut Pro (*www. apple.com/finalcutstudio*), a professional, non-linear editing program that has many editing capabilities beyond the needs of the novice user. Final Cut offers more control over effects and transitions and allows the user to more accurately edit video than its free counterparts. Final Cut is used by professional journalists as well as for big budget Hollywood movies and is available for Mac computers only. Final Cut Pro is a part of the Final Cut Studio software package which also comes with additional programs for professional audio editing, graphic design, and more. Final Cut Express, a less expensive version of Final Cut, has almost all the features of Final Cut Pro, but does not include the additional applications packaged with Final Cut Studio. Also, Final Cut Express is geared toward amateur and novice editors and does not have many of the advanced options as Final Cut Pro. Both programs share the same layout and functions has.

Final Cut Pro

Avid Media Composer (*www.avid.com*), often referred to simply as Avid, is a non-linear, computer-based video editing system that is popular in many broadcast television newsrooms and is available for both Mac and PC computers. Just as some computer users prefer Macs and others prefer PCs, there are some video editors who prefer Final Cut and those who prefer Avid. Both editing systems can create transitions, effects, titles and other advanced edits. Final Cut, however, is easier for beginners to master. The program has many advanced features that novice users don't ever have to use to understand how it works.

Avid Media Composer

The video editing software you use should depend on the level of expertise of the editor as well as the budget of the newsroom. Beginners should stick with iMovie, while seasoned editors will appreciate the robust features available in professional video editors like Avid and Final Cut. Other popular professional video editing software include Adobe Premiere (*www.adobe.com/products/premiere*) and Sony Vegas Pro (*www.sonycreativesoftware.com/vegaspro*). Many of the previously mentioned video editing systems differ in the advanced features they offer, but all share similar features and components.

Most non-linear video editing systems include a *timeline*, an area of the program where video and audio clips are laid out and assembled into a sequence and where most of the basic editing happens. The timeline stretches horizontally and can include as many clips as the video requires.

A timeline contains individual *tracks* or layers that allow the editor to stack video and audio clips on top of one another so they appear at the same time in the final video. In most programs, video and audio recorded at the same time can be separated and added to separate tracks. This means you can layer ambient sound on top of video and audio from a single interview and all three tracks will be played at the same time, allowing the viewer to both hear and see the video as well as the ambient sound. Professional video editing software allows for a seemingly infinite number of tracks for adding and manipulating many layers of sound and video. If you plan to edit complex video that requires multiple video and audio tracks, you should select advanced video editing software that offers this level of flexibility. Some video editing programs also allow the editor to import audio such as MP3 files for use in the video.

The *scrubber* or *playhead* (the terms are sometimes used interchangeably), is a line used to indicate where to start playing the video or where to make a cut. The line that stretches vertically across the timeline is sometimes referred to as the scrubber, while the marker on top of the scrubber is called the playhead. The scrubber is also used as a selection tool to highlight or select portions of video or audio. Video editing programs also include separate controls to start, stop, pause, fast forward, and rewind the video assembled on the timeline or individual clips.

Most programs also include an area where video and audio clips and sometimes images are stored for use during the editing process. In Final Cut this area is called the *browser*, in iMovie it is the *shelf*, and in Avid it is called the *bin*. Media stored in this area should be labeled to help identify the content of the clips. Every video editing program includes a screen where you can view your edited video, preview changes as they are made, or view video clips once they are imported to the program. In Final Cut this area is called the *canvas*, in iMovie it is the *monitor*.

 To see a digital video editing program in action
go to **djhandbook.net/videoediting**

Video files can be very large and can take up a significant amount of space on the computer. Many professional video editors store video files on an *external hard drive*, a portable storage system used to store large media without using space on the computer.

The first step in video editing is *logging*, the process of watching the footage you've shot and extracting and labeling clips according to their content. Often, you will shoot much more video than you will use in the final piece. Logging helps separate the best video clips from the rest of the footage. Logging can be done by hand by creating a written log of the best parts of the video or electronically using a video editing program like Final Cut. Instead of importing the entire video directly into the program, some video editing systems allow the editor to electronically select and extract clips that can be used in the video. These clips don't have to be precise, just a rough edit of what you'd like to include.

Whether it is done by hand or electronically, logging requires the editor to identify the *in* and *out points*, the beginning and end of each clip that will be extracted from the video. Finding these points is as easy as consulting the *time code*, a feature found on many video cameras that assigns a specific time marker to each frame of the video. Time code is represented in hours, minutes, seconds, and frames, and is usually formatted as HH:MM:SS:FF. A full time code notation looks like the numbers on a digital clock, except for the last two digits.

1:24:18:12

The above number is read as 1 hour, 24 minutes, 18 seconds, and 12 frames. You can usually view the time code in the camera when you record video. As you record, the video camera notes the time code for each frame and displays it in the viewfinder or on the LCD screen. Time code makes it possible to make precise edits, down to a single frame. When logging lengthy interviews, look for *soundbites*, short phrases or sentences that capture the essence of what the speaker has said. Soundbites reduce the time required for the speaker to make his or her point. Logging video can be a tedious process, but can make locating and organizing usable clips easier.

The second step after logging clips is *capturing* video or transferring it from the camera and importing into the computer or editing software. Logging and capturing clips instead of the whole video saves time and reduces the amount of video that is imported into the program.

The fundamental process of video editing is importing video clips and arranging them into a proper sequence on the timeline. When you edit video, start by creating a *rough cut*, an approximation of how the clips will be edited and arranged. You will usually love most of the footage you shot, but will have to part with much of it to create your final video. Once you create a rough cut, you can make more precise edits and shape the video into the final product.

Pacing, the length of time between each new shot, can set the tone for the video. Video with a fast pace and a shorter time between shots can create a feeling of excitement or energy. Slow pacing can be used to convey a sense of calm, peace, or sadness. Video is often limited to just a few minutes and shots shouldn't last too long, regardless of the pacing. Online viewers have short attention spans compared to television audiences who are used to watching video programming for hours on end. For example, a 20-second shot in a one-minute video is often too long and is in danger of losing the viewer's attention. If an important clip or shot such as a lengthy interview lasts too long, break it up with b-roll to keep the viewer engaged in the story and not staring blankly at the screen. Include only what is necessary to tell the story and avoid repeating information. If a point is made more than once or the same action occurs repeatedly, find the clip that best conveys the sentiment or action and cut the rest.

The audio of a video project is just as important as the video itself and editors should pay close attention to how a video sounds as well as how it looks. Always use headphones when you edit video to monitor the audio quality and listen for any audio problems. If a video clip is good, but the audio is terrible, the audio must be separated from the clip or, if this is not an option, the entire video clip should be thrown out. You don't always have to match video with the audio that was recorded at the same time, but you should not blend video and audio that were not recorded in the same session. For example, for a video story about a protest, it is okay to match video of the crowd with similar audio that was recorded later in the protest. It is not okay to match video of one protest with audio from another or to add sound effects of a chanting crowd.

After you arrange your video and audio on the timeline, you can also add titles and credits. Each speaker or interviewee should be identified by name and title when they first appear in the video using a *lower third*. A lower third is like a caption for video and is so named because the identifying text appears in the bottom third of the screen. The name of the person usually appears on one line and their title or other identification appears immediately below.

Most video editing programs let the editor add transitions between video clips such as fades and dissolves. There are a variety of special effects that can be added to video, including fancy transitions and flashy graphics. For professional news video, these should be used sparingly. Fancy effects are usually the sign of amateur or homemade video.

A lower third

When you are finished editing and all your video and audio is assembled into a complete story, unplug your headphones, turn off your computer speakers, and watch your video without the audio. Noted film director Alfred Hitchcock famously said if you can watch a film without audio and still understand the story, then the film is well made. Watch your video and see if you can follow the storyline and look out for any technical glitches, mistakes, or inconsistencies. Then, put on a pair of headphones, close your eyes, and listen to the audio by itself. You can often miss audio problems when you're also concentrating on the video.

Video editing takes practice so start by editing home movies or any video you've shot in your spare time. The more often you edit, the more natural the process will become, allowing you to more quickly edit and publish your video.

 For video editing tutorials and resources
go to **djhandbook.net/videoediting**

Posting and sharing video

Once your video is edited, it should be saved in one of a few common file formats, depending on its intended use. There are several types of video files, the most common used by digital journalists are MOV, a video file format for QuickTime movies and MPEG, a compressed video file format. Other formats include AVI, a compressed video file developed by Microsoft, and MP4, a compressed multimedia file format developed by Apple, noted for its compatibility with the iPod. Compression strips information away from the original video file to create a smaller file size, while uncompressed video is larger and takes more time to load or download when posted online.

The easiest way to share a video file is to upload the file to the web and create a link to the online video file. Depending on the format of the file, the web browser creates an unstyled video player that allows the visitor to view the file. However, most online video is made available through an *embedded video player*. Embedded video players can take various shapes and forms, but often have core functions such as the ability to play, pause, stop, and adjust the volume of the audio, and can include a timeline that identifies the progression and total time of the video file. These players are often created with Flash, the animation software outlined in Chapter 10.

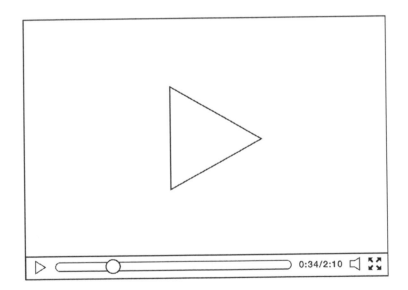

The layout of a typical embedded video player

Some news sites post online video to a dedicated video *channel*, a single web page that contains several video clips embedded on the same page. Many television stations use video channels to make clips or entire broadcasts available online for viewers to watch at their leisure. For example, airings of the cable comedy-news show "The Daily Show with Jon Stewart" (*www.thedailyshow.com*) are available online in their entirety. The site receives hundreds of thousands of online viewers in addition to its traditional television audience, according to the market research firm comScore. The online videos give viewers an opportunity to catch up on shows they may have missed or to skip the original television broadcast altogether.

In addition to posting their video content on their own sites, some media organizations also post video to social networking/video sharing sites like YouTube (outlined in detail in Chapter 9). More than 60 percent of adult internet users have watched video online, according to a 2010 survey by the Pew Research Center, and YouTube is one of the most visited sites on the web with millions of daily visitors. Posting video to third-party websites opens up content to online viewers who may not visit an actual news site. Video posted to these sites usually includes a link back to the website of the news organization.

Many news sites have their own proprietary tools for embedding video, so consult your newsroom's web producer for more information. If you don't have access to an embeddable video player, online video sharing sites like YouTube (*www.youtube.com*) and Vimeo (*www.vimeo.com*) allow anyone to upload video and post it anywhere on the web using an embeddable video player.

Video posted on the web should be accompanied by a text summary that describes what the viewer will see. A brief description helps the online visitor decide if the video is something they are interested in and makes it more likely that search engines like Google that cannot "see" the video will present the video in search results. A summary should include keywords that describe the content of the video, which in turn helps search engine users who have entered the same keywords find the video.

A lot of work goes into creating online video, including shooting, storyboarding, editing, and publishing, so make sure potential viewers know it exists by creating prominent links to your video content on your website.

WEB DESIGN

CHAPTER EIGHT

In the many years that online news sites have existed, a large percentage of reporters and journalists have had their work published and posted online without actually knowing how a news website works or understanding any of the technical elements that power it. In addition to traditional reporting duties, journalists now are being asked to learn the basic computer skills required to post their stories online. Reporters are sometimes asked to *code* or add computer language to their story to make it presentable for the web. When a story or other news content is posted to the web, special computer coding is added to the text or other media to indicate how it should be displayed in a web browser. In the past, a newsroom web producer or site manager would perform this task for the journalist after the story was edited and filed. Now, many newsrooms require journalists to code their own their stories and post them directly to the web.

Some tech-savvy journalists also combine complex programming with traditional journalism to use the capabilities of the web to elevate news stories. Understanding the basics of computer languages and how they affect online journalism is now a necessary skill for working in a digital newsroom.

Coding does not come naturally for many journalists and requires a different kind of thinking. The left brain, which controls logic and analysis, is used for skills like computer programming. The right brain controls intuition and creative thought, skills that are necessary to succeed in journalism. Because journalists are more likely to be right-brain thinkers, asking a writer to code is basically asking them to rethink the way they think. For many journalists, learning coding is not as easy as picking up a book or attending a class. This is not to say it cannot be done. To successfully acquire both skills, you must tap into both hemispheres of the brain and think both analytically and creatively. Journalism and computer coding may require two different skill sets, but to succeed in a digital news environment, you should learn the basic computer skills required to post your content online and be able to speak fluently about the web publishing process. You don't have to be an expert, but at the very least you should know what happens to your story after it is filed.

Content management systems

Most journalists do not build web pages or sites from scratch. Instead, they use a *content management system* or CMS, a web-based computer application that lets users upload, organize, and publish online content without affecting the design or functionality of the site. Using a CMS, newsroom staff such as reporters and editors can post or edit online stories without building the web pages themselves or handling complex programming languages. Most online content, including stories, multimedia, and any sort of web page that appears on a news site is posted using a CMS, which is usually accessed online and looks like an online form. The user simply fills out the form with information about the story or article, including the text of the story, a headline, the author, and a dateline. Some content management systems allow users to create links and embed photos and other media such as video and audio. When the form is submitted, the CMS creates a single web page that mirrors the design and layout of the news site and contains all the content submitted in the form.

CMS

Navigation	
	Title
	Author
	Date
	Content
	B *I* <u>U</u> ☰ ☰ ☰ ☰ -- Styles -- ⇕ -- Paragraph -- ⇕
	Upload image (Browse...)

The layout of a typical content management system

Using a CMS is similar to handing content over to a page designer for a print publication. After all the stories are written and the photos are selected, it is the page designer's job to lay them out on the page, decide what order and section they should appear in, and make sure the layout follows the newsroom's style. A CMS is like a digital page designer and automatically creates and lays out pages according to specifications set by the newsroom's web developer(s) or designer. The hundreds, sometimes thousands, of pages that make up a news website are often governed by a CMS, which standardizes the visual appearance of various elements such as the size and color of text, the width of columns, and the placement of images.

Most professional news organizations use a CMS to organize and publish online content. There are many types of content management systems with various functions and features and no two are the same. Popular content management systems include Drupal, Joomla, and WordPress, though there are various systems used in newsrooms.

A content management system is used not only to publish web pages, but to categorize them as well. CMS users can add *tags* or keywords to classify their content and organize it within the site. This tagging system can be used to create *landing pages* or web pages within a website that contain or link to similar content. For example, news sites can organize their content by subject or topic such as "Business" or "Sports" and have all the related articles that fall under those categories appear on a single landing page. Landing pages are the online equivalent of newspaper sections and can be automatically populated using a CMS. A content management system can also classify content by author, which allows each reporter or contributor to have his or her own web page that contains all their content or stories.

A CMS can also be used to upload files from a computer to a website. Photographers, for example, can use a CMS to upload images and reporters can sometimes upload or embed multimedia content such as video or audio files. Different systems have different settings and, depending on the newsroom, some CMS users are not allowed to post media other than text. Instead of using CMS to upload media files, some news sites use an FTP tool. FTP, short for File Transfer Protocol, is used to upload or transfer files to a *server*, the online space where all the files of a website are stored and accessed. A server is like a file cabinet that can store files and an FTP is like the person who retrieves and stores files in the file cabinet. When you transfer a file to the server, the FTP makes a copy of the computer file and places that copy in a selected folder.

There are many different FTP tools, some of which are accessed online and others that are computer software such as FileZilla (*www.filezilla-project.org*), a downloadable FTP program. An FTP tool usually requires a password to access the website and the files that are stored on the server. Because of its sensitivity, many reporters and editors do not have access to the FTP and instead only interact with a CMS.

Content management systems are often used so journalists have to do as little coding as possible. Many novice digital journalists learn web design using computer programs like Dreamweaver to create web pages and other online content from the ground up. This is great for learning the web design process, but the average journalist isn't required to build their online stories from scratch.

Most journalists who work for a professional news organization use a content management system daily or have at least encountered one. If you haven't yet worked with a CMS, you can use the blogging tool WordPress (*www.wordpress. com*) to explore how a CMS works. WordPress can create individual articles with headlines, text, and tags and like many other blogging tools is actually a specific type of CMS.

 For resources and tutorials on content management systems, go to **djhandbook.net/cms**

HTML

Content management systems make it less likely that reporters will encounter complex programming languages, but many systems require journalists to learn basic coding to format and post their stories online. Often this is done using HTML, a basic computer language that is the backbone of most websites and online content. HTML, short for HyperText Markup Language, controls how a website or page is structured and, in a CMS, is sometimes added to the text of an online story to format what would otherwise appear online as a plain block of text.

HTML is based on a system of "tags" that tells the web browser how to display online elements such as text, links, and images. HTML tags are used to create the various text effects that appear on websites, including **bold** and *italic* text and to add links or images within the text. HTML tags are keywords, usually one or several letters surrounded by angle brackets. For example, the bold tag is written as <b>. The letter "b" indicates the text should be bold and is surrounded by angle brackets to form the tag. Tags usually come in pairs. The first tag in the pair is the *opening tag* and is placed at the beginning of the text to be formatted. The second tag is the *end* or *closing tag* and usually includes a forward slash (/) that indicates that it is the end of that particular bit of the code. The closing tag is placed at the end of the text. For example, to indicate that a specific part of text should be bold, include the opening tag, then the text, then the closing tag. In this case, <b>Man Walks on Moon</b> would appear in the web browser as **Man Walks on Moon**.

A *browser*, a computer application used to access the internet (e.g. Firefox, Internet Explorer, or Safari), recognizes the HTML and formats the text according to the tag. The online reader never sees the HTML, but does see its effects. There are a few basic HTML tags that online journalists and web producers use to format text, especially when using a CMS. The following are some of the most frequently used tags in online news.

Bold text, which is thicker than normal text, is often used to format subheads or to indicate speakers in an online Q&A. The <b> tag, as previously mentioned, creates bold text. For example, to create the following text with HTML, bold tags should be added to the text at the beginning and end of the text you want to format:

<b>Daily Times:</b> How are you today?
<b>Interviewee:</b> I'm doing fine, thanks.

Daily Times: How are you today?
Interviewee: I'm doing fine, thanks.

Italic text is used to indicate foreign words, to add emphasis, or to indicate the presence another speaker. To create italic text, use the <i> tag. Place the opening tag before the text you want to format and the closing tag after.

No one said you <i>shouldn't</i> do that.

No one said you *shouldn't* do that.

You can also add emphasis to text using the <strong> and <em> tags. These tags are used the same way as the <b> and <i> tags and, depending on the style of the website, are used to create bold or italic text.

When coding online text, it is sometimes necessary to indicate the beginning and end of a paragraph. Paragraph breaks are created with the <p> tag. By placing <p> (the opening tag) at the beginning of a block of text and </p> (the closing tag) after, the browser will create a break with space before and after the text. For example, to create two paragraphs from a single block of text, add the opening and closing tags before and after each paragraph.

<p>Many people meet their loved ones at the airport. Sue Smith is no exception.</p><p>Her parents frequently travel by plane and she is always waiting by the curb to pick them up.</p>

Many people meet at the airport to greet their loved ones. Sue Smith is no exception.

Her parents frequently travel by plane and she is always waiting by the curb to pick them up.

The <br /> tag creates a single line break in the text and has no closing tag. For example, "I need a break
from coding" will appear online as

I need a break
from coding

The <img> tag is used for embedding images in a web page and, unlike the <b>, <i>, and <p> tags, has no closing tag. The <img> tag must include "src" which tells the browser where the image exists online. For example, <img src="http://www.djhandbook.net/image.jpg" /> tells the browser to display the image found at the web address between the parentheses.

Additional code can be added to the <img> tag to indicate additional properties of the image such as width and height. <img src="http://www.djhandbook. net/image.jpg" width="150" height="100" /> for example, tells the browser that the image is 150 pixels wide and 100 pixels high.

You can also include an *alt* attribute, which is used as alternative text if the image is not available and is also useful for blind web visitors who use screen readers to browse the internet. A screen reader reads aloud the content of the website and instead of an image will read the alt text. For example, if you include an image of an umbrella, the alt attribute should include the word "umbrella" between the parentheses to indicate to the screen reader that the image is of an umbrella, as in the example below.

```
<img src="http://www.djhandbook.net/umbrella.jpg" width="150"
height="100" alt="umbrella" />
```

The <a> tag is used to create links that, when clicked, direct readers to other web pages or sites. Just as the <img> tag uses "src" to indicate where the image exists online, the <a> tag uses "href" to specify the URL or web address of the page or site that the visitor will be directed to. For example, to create a link to *The Digital Journalist's Handbook* website (*www.djhandbook.net*), the link written in HTML appears as

```
<a href="http://www.djhandbook.net">Digital Journalist's Handbook</a>
```

The web address is placed between the parentheses and the text is placed between the opening and closing tags. When the link is displayed online the reader only sees the text of the link, as in the example below:

Digital Journalist's Handbook

Text is the most common way to create a link, but you can also create links using images. When the image is clicked, the reader is taken to a website included in the parentheses after the href attribute. To create a link for an image, place the <img> tag between the opening and closing <a> tag as in the example below.

```
<a href="http://www.djhandbook.net"><img src="http://www.
website.com/image.jpg" /></a>
```

You can also use links to direct online readers to an e-mail address. Instead of placing a web address in between parentheses, include "mailto:" then the e-mail address you want to link to.

```
<a href="mailto:person@website.com">person@website.com</a>
```

When the reader clicks the link, their default e-mail program will create a message to be sent to the selected e-mail address.

Sometimes, journalists create bulleted lists, like the one below:

- The sun is bright
- The sky is blue
- The water is clear

To create such as list, including the line breaks, indentations, and bullets, use a combination of the <ul> and <li> tags. The opening <ul> tag is placed at the beginning of the list. The <li> tag precedes each list item and adds a bullet at the beginning of each line. The </li> closing tag is placed at the end of each line and the </ul> closing tag is included once at the end of the list. The previous text would be coded like this:

```
<ul>
<li>The sun is bright</li>
<li>The sky is blue</li>
<li>The water is clear</li>
</ul>
```

To create a list with numbers instead of dots, replace the <ul> tag with the <ol> tag.

```
<ol>
<li>The sun is bright</li>
<li>The sky is blue</li>
<li>The water is clear</li>
</ol>
```

There are many more HTML tags, but the tags mentioned here are the ones the average journalist will encounter when using a CMS or other web development program. On the next page is a chart of all the tags and their uses, plus a few other tags you may encounter.

HTML TAGS

TAG	DESCRIPTION
`<A>`	Defines an anchor (usually for a link)
`<B>`	Defines bold text
`<BLOCKQUOTE>`	Defines a long quotation
`<BODY>`	Defines the document's body
` `	Defines a single line break
`<CENTER>`	Defines centered text
`<DIV>`	Defines a section in a document
`<EM>`	Defines emphasized text
`<HEAD>`	Defines information about the document
`<HR />`	Defines a horizontal line
`<HTML>`	Defines an HTML document
`<I>`	Defines italic text
`<IMG />`	Defines an image
`<LI>`	Defines a list item
`<OL>`	Defines an ordered list
`<P>`	Defines a paragraph
`<S>`	Defines strikethrough text
`<STRIKE>`	Defines strikethrough text
`<STRONG>`	Defines strong text
`<TABLE>`	Defines a table
`<TD>`	Defines a cell in a table
`<TH>`	Defines a header cell in a table
`<TITLE>`	Defines the title of a document
`<TR>`	Defines a row in a table
`<U>`	Defines underlined text
`<UL>`	Defines an unordered list

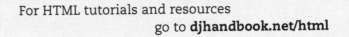

For HTML tutorials and resources
go to **djhandbook.net/html**

Often journalists need to include special characters in their stories such as the ó in "La Nación" or the ñ in "señorita." Simply copying and pasting the character into a CMS or other web authoring system such as Dreamweaver will display jumbled text instead of the character. Instead, brief bits of HTML code or "entities" should be inserted into the copy to ensure the character is read correctly by the browser. An HTML entity is a keyword or number preceded by an ampersand and followed by a semicolon. For example, the "ó" in "La Nación" would instead be written as "ó" and the text would be as "La Nación" with no space between the entity and the rest of the text. Online readers will see "La Nación" and not the code.

For a list of commonly used HTML entities
go to **djhandbook.net/entities**

CSS

HTML controls the structure and formatting of a website or page, but CSS, another coding language, indicates how it is styled. CSS, short for Cascading Style Sheets, governs how HTML elements such as text and links appear on the page, including the size and color of text and the width and position of columns. For example, a basic link without any style added to it appears in the web browser as blue, underlined text. CSS allows the web designer to alter the styling of all the links that appear on the site. The link on the right is styled in a different text size, font, and the underline has been removed. No matter the styling, both links would take the reader to the same website indicated by the HTML.

<u>**This is an unstyled link**</u>

This is a link styled with CSS

CSS can be coded directly into an HTML file adjacent to the content, but is more commonly included in an "external" *stylesheet*, a separate file that controls the look of an entire website and its individual pages, including the formatting of the text, the colors that appear on the page, and more. News sites can contain hundreds of thousands of pages and to change each one individually would require a lot of time and effort. By making a change to the stylesheet, a web producer can change how every page on a site appears. The CSS stylesheet is what powers the design and layout of pages created by a content management system and is stored online separate from other online files.

In newsrooms and other major companies, the CSS stylesheet is a sensitive document and is not usually accessible by the majority of newsroom staff, even by some web producers. Journalists, however, should be aware of what a stylesheet is and how it controls the design of a website.

 For further information on CSS, including examples and tutorials, go to **djhandbook.net/css**

Journalism and programming

As online journalism becomes more advanced, some newsrooms have hired special staff that have both strong web development skills and a strong background in journalism. The new crop of journo-programmers are often fluent in HTML and CSS, as well as more advanced programming languages such as XML, PHP, or Ruby on Rails (discussed further in Chapter 10). Online news stories backed by complex coding range from interactive stories to dynamic, data-driven web applications and databases.

There are many different types of journo-programmers, some of whom are more fluent in one skill or the other but understand how technology can enhance journalism. These skills are being used to create even more inventive forms of online journalism such as EveryBlock, a *hyperlocal* news site that uses data instead of traditional reporting to document local news, and PolitiFact, a site that uses online databases to track the statements of political candidates.

EveryBlock (*www.everyblock.com*), launched in 2008, aggregates publicly available

EveryBlock (*www.everyblock.com*), launched in 2008, aggregates publicly available data such as local crime statistics, real estate information, business licenses, and news feeds. Visitors to the site can find news near them by entering their address or postal code and see information such as nearby crimes and restaurant inspections and view the data on interactive charts and maps. The site covers several major U.S. cities, including New York, Los Angeles, and San Francisco, and allows visitors to search for information in their neighborhood or even on their block, hence the name. Much of the information featured on the site is gathered by contacting various local and civic organizations and is information that is already available to the public. EveryBlock's focus on location-based data is very different from the traditional narratives and stories that are synonymous with journalism and is made possible by a team of web programmers and designers who also have an instinct for local news.

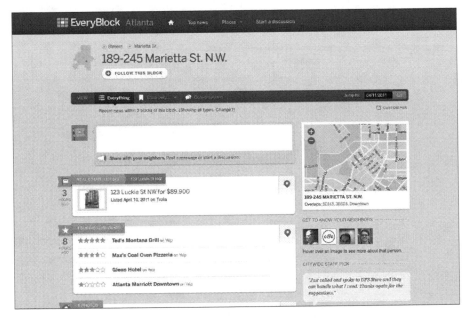

EveryBlock (www.everyblock.com)

PolitiFact (*www.politifact.com*), a Pulitzer Prize-winning online project by the St. Petersburg Times, analyzes speeches, television ads, and interviews of politicians and political players and determines whether the claims they make are accurate or false. The findings are presented as the "Truth-O-Meter," an online graphic that rates claims and attacks as "True," "Mostly True," "Half True," "Barely True," and "False." The most outrageous statements are given the lowest rating, "Pants on Fire."

PolitiFact was originally developed to fact-check claims made by candidates during the 2008 U.S. election. The site now assesses how the current presidential administration is delivering on its promises with the "Obameter," a database of more than 500 promises that U.S. President Barack Obama made during his political campaign. PolitiFact lists the sources for each analysis and helps readers understand American politics, but in a less traditional, more data-driven way. The site mixes traditional investigative reporting with advanced programming and online databases to create inventive online journalism that moves the craft beyond the traditional text story.

PolitiFact (www.politifact.com)

While the advanced technical skills that power EveryBlock and PolitiFact are often beyond the skill set of the average journalist, both reporters and editors should at least know what is possible with advanced programming languages and understand how they can enhance traditional reporting. True journo-programmers with equal strengths in both professions are rare as it still a very new role in the newsroom, but with programming being taught in newsrooms and universities, even more should emerge in the coming years. Journalists often work with traditional programmers to create complex online journalism, so it is important to, at the very least, understand the capabilities of advanced web development. You'll find you are more likely to be invested in the technical process of creating complex online stories if you have an idea of how these tools can shape and contribute to online journalism.

SOCIAL NETWORKING

CHAPTER NINE

Social networks are online communities where users communicate and interact with one another using the web as a platform. There are hundreds of online social networks dedicated to a variety of interests, hobbies, and geographic locations or cater to specific audiences — everyone from moms to sports fans to pet owners. General interest social networks such as Facebook, MySpace, Twitter, and YouTube each attract millions of active users and daily visitors. Social networks are built around the concept of "friends," online connections that can be anyone from a next-door neighbor to someone on the other side of the world. Online friends may never meet in person, but, because of the global reach of the internet, can interact with one another online.

Many social networkers use the sites to share and comment on news stories and by doing so have transformed the way journalism is distributed on the web. In the early days of online journalism, web audiences had to visit an actual news website to view recent news stories and could share what they read with a few people at a time using e-mail, instant messaging, or other forms of personal communication. Social networks allow news audiences to share what they've read with hundreds or even millions of like-minded readers at a time and to discover news stories that are relevant to them without visiting an online news site directly. Instead of relying on a news organization to decide what news stories are important, many social network users rely on the wisdom of their peers and are more likely to read a news story or other online content if it is recommended or shared by a friend or other trusted person. Social networks also allow web users to share breaking news that is happening around them without waiting for a traditional news organization to report it. For all these reasons, it is important for journalists to be active members of social networks, both to be aware of what people are discussing online and to interact with their communities and audience.

In the golden age of journalism, reporters could hide behind their bylines and their desks, but in the digital age are now expected to interact with the communities they cover — both on and offline. Journalists use social networks to share information with readers about news relevant to their beat and establish relationships and ongoing conversations surrounding the news. Reporters also use social networks as a source for potential news stories or to monitor growing trends.

There are as many social networks as there are hobbies and interests. However, each social network has its own unique features and attracts different types of online users. Many social networks have common functions such as *tagging*, or classifying articles or links with relevant keywords, and *social bookmarking*, using the internet to save and share websites and online content. The following social networks — Twitter, Facebook, Digg, YouTube, StumbleUpon, and Flickr — are some of the most popular social networks among both internet users and journalists.

Twitter

Twitter (*www.twitter.com*) is a popular online social network where members view and post short messages called "tweets" to a network of contacts. Tweets, which must be 140 characters or less, can be posted to the web using the Twitter website, from a mobile device such as a cell phone, or using a third-party tool or site. There are many different Twitter users — including journalists, teenagers, celebrities, and major corporations — and many ways to use the site. Twitter users can talk with friends, share their thoughts on current events, receive updates on latest news, and more. The type of interaction and conversation you have on Twitter is entirely dependent on the people in your network.

Twitter (www.twitter.com)

To get started on Twitter, you must first set up a profile that includes your name, biographical information, and optionally a web address and image of yourself. You must also select a *username*, an online alias that can be any combination of letters and numbers. Usernames are usually a variation of the person's actual name. For example, CNN anchor Anderson Cooper's Twitter username is "andersoncooper." Once you set up a profile, you can start posting tweets to your *feed*, a collection of messages posted to the site. Because tweets are limited to 140 characters, messages posted to Twitter must be brief, usually no longer than a sentence or two. Many Twitter users work within this restriction by making more concise statements and using abbreviations or shortened words. This form of online communication is called *microblogging*, or writing a regular series of very short posts.

Twitter users can read and receive messages posted by another user by "following" them. Following another person is as easy as clicking a button in his or her profile that allows you to subscribe to their Twitter feed. When two users follow each other, they become "friends." Twitter users can also "unfollow" or unsubscribe to another person's tweets at any time. A Twitter user's feed can be accessed by adding their username to the end of the Twitter web address. For example, the tweets of the user "marksluckie," author of this book, can be viewed at www.twitter.com/*marksluckie* Messages posted to the site can be viewed by anyone who visits your profile unless you mark it as private, a setting that lets only those people who you allow view your profile and see your messages.

Twitter users can reply or respond to another user's tweet by including that person's username at the beginning of the message, preceded by the @ symbol. For example, to direct a message to the user "marksluckie," begin the tweet with "@marksluckie." The @ symbol is also used to refer to a particular Twitter user in a tweet. For example, the message "Watching @oprah on TV" refers to Twitter user and media mogul Oprah Winfrey. Instead of a public back-and-forth exchange, users can also send "direct messages" or DMs, a tweet sent directly from one person to another. Direct messages function like e-mail and do not appear in either person's public Twitter feed.

Twitter users can also *retweet* or repost a message sent by another user. Retweeting another user's message is a way to share what they posted with your own followers and is a common way news stories are shared on Twitter. There is more than one way to retweet a message, but it is often done by copying and pasting the original message or some variation of the message in a new tweet and including the abbreviation "RT," followed by the username of the original poster. The total message would be written like in the example below:

A retweet posted to Twitter

"RT" signifies the message was originally posted by the Twitter user "MSNBC" and is followed by the original tweet. The original message does not have to be repeated word for word. You can also add your own commentary or simply restate the idea in a different way. You can also retweet by including the word "via" and the username of the person at the end of the tweet (e.g. "via @marksluckie"), which lets other users know how you found the information included in the message. Twitter users can also repost another user's tweet by clicking the "Retweet" button found under every Twitter post.

Twitter users can also identify the subject of a tweet using one or more *hashtags*. Hashtags begin with the # sign and are followed by a keyword (e.g. "#sports" or "#news") and can be included anywhere in a tweet. Hashtags make it easier to group or search for tweets posted about a particular subject or topic. Hashtags are often used by attendees or observers of an event, such as a conference or sporting match, to discuss what is happening and their feelings or reactions to the event. For example, attendees and viewers of the annual Wimbledon tennis tournament use the hashtag "#wimbledon" to share their thoughts and discuss the event on Twitter. You can search for tweets that include hashtags or particular keywords using Twitter's search page (*search.twitter.com*).

Traditional media often use hashtags to solicit and gather comments from Twitter users. For example, to direct a message to the cable network Current TV, Twitter users can include the hashtag "#current" in their tweets. Anyone searching for the #current hashtag will find all the tweets sent to the news organization. Hashtags can also be used to bring attention to a cause. To protest the lack of coverage of the 2009 voter protests in Iran on CNN, many Twitter users included the hashtag "#cnnfail" in their messages to encourage the network to increase its coverage of the issue. After the hashtag was introduced and circulated by thousands of Twitter users, there was a noted increase of Iran coverage on the network.

Tweets can only contain text — Twitter users can't include pictures, video, or other media in their tweets, but can include a link to them. Some longer web addresses can easily exceed the 140-character limit, so Twitter automatically converts web addresses sent through the site into *shortened URLs* — links that compress the full website address into a smaller one that uses fewer characters. For example, a long address like "http://www.longwebsitename.com/equally-long-web-page.html" can be converted to a shorter address like "http://bit.ly/ShorTer." When someone clicks the link, they are directed to the correct website.

Many Twitter users do not use the Twitter site itself to post or read tweets, but instead use one of the many third-party tools based on Twitter technology that expand the features of the service. These third-party tools include TwitPic (*www.twitpic.com*), a site where users can upload photos and post links to them in their tweets, and Twitterfeed (*www.twitterfeed.com*), which lets Twitter users automatically post the content of their RSS feed in their Twitter feed.

Before you begin following other Twitter users, you should first post a few tweets that represent what you will tweet about to give potential followers a reason to follow you back. If you follow someone but haven't yet posted any tweets, the person is usually less motivated to follow you. Also, avoid following hundreds or thousands of people at once. Twitter users who are following a significantly larger number of people and have a relatively low number of users following them back are sometimes mistaken for spammers. Twitter spammers follow many people at once in hopes of driving traffic to their website or product.

With millions of users sharing their lives and the events around them, Twitter has become a sort of global wire service where both average citizens and news organizations contribute to a worldwide stream of news. Twitter users can consult the site's *trending topics*, or the most discussed topics on the site, to get a feel of what Twitter users are talking about or to stay abreast of breaking news. Trending topics are featured on the Twitter homepage and in the sidebar of the Twitter website.

For journalists and news media, Twitter is a great way to share news as it happens and to immediately broadcast stories to millions of Twitter users. Many mainstream news media have at least one Twitter account and many more have reporters and staff who use the site to talk with and listen to their audience. News personalities like MSNBC's Rachel Maddow (@maddow), BBC Radio's Richard Bacon (@richardpbacon), and CNN's Wolf Blitzer (@wolfblitzercnn), each of whom have millions of followers, use Twitter to share news and engage in active conversations with their followers. Some journalists use the site to pose questions to or solicit opinions from their followers and friends that be included in their reporting. Broadcast news media like Current TV collect Twitter comments or replies and display them during on-air broadcasts. The tweets are often pre-selected and are similar to the "Letters to the editor" section in traditional newspapers.

Many major news organizations on Twitter have several different Twitter feeds dedicated to a specific section or topic that the newsroom covers. For example, the *Chicago Tribune* has many different Twitter accounts, including feeds dedicated to Business (*twitter.com/ChiTribBusiness*), Sports (*twitter.com/ChiTribSports*), and Travel (*twitter.com/ChiTribTravel*), as well as separate accounts for many *Tribune* reporters and columnists. The *Tribune* and many other news organizations also have Twitter directories on their main website to make it easier for readers or viewers to find the Twitter account of every staff member or news section in one place. Such pages often include links for online visitors to follow each Twitter feed and a feed of recent tweets from the newsroom.

 For a guide to news organizations on Twitter
go to **djhandbook.net/newsontwitter**

Journalists can use Twitter to enhance their reporting by following people in their community or audience and follow discussions relevant to their beat. Third-party tools like Nearby Tweets (*www.nearbytweets.com*) make it possible to locate Twitter users in a geographic area by searching for a specific location or postal code. Sites like Breaking Tweets (*www.breakingtweets.com*) indicate what news topics are *trending*, or are increasingly discussed by Twitter users. Twitter is also a useful tool for connecting with other journalists to share ideas on stories or coverage.

Twitter is commonly used as a tool for posting and sharing breaking news and, because of this, has significantly altered the traditional news cycle. News is often posted to Twitter as it happens and quickly spreads among the site's users, often within minutes of its occurrence and long before the story is covered by traditional news outlets. Twitter solidified its status as a tool for breaking news during the 2008 bombings in Mumbai when witnesses and victims used the site to report the attacks as they happened and before major news outlets made it to the scene. Now, both average citizens and journalists regularly use the site to instantly share breaking news with others.

Journalists and other Twitter users unaffiliated with a media organization also use the site to provide coverage or analysis of live events, often using just a cell phone or other mobile device to do so. Many reporters, for example, live-tweeted the inauguration of U.S. President Barack Obama as the event occurred. Some journalists also use Twitter to share real-time coverage of legal proceedings.

Reporters from newspapers like *The Orange County Register* and the *Wichita Eagle* have used Twitter to share live updates of local trials as they happened.

In some cases, it is unwise to tweet breaking news without the oversight of an editor or a supervisor who can fact-check the information before it is released. Unconfirmed facts and rumor can spread quickly on Twitter. Many more people may see an incorrect tweet before they see a later correction. On Twitter, as with all journalism, it is better to be accurate than fast.

Twitter has millions of users that can potentially be converted into traffic to a news site. If a link to a story or article is retweeted many times, it can spread quickly among Twitter users and be seen by hundreds of thousands of online readers. However, because of the fleeting nature of Twitter, often these are short bursts of traffic that don't last long. Some traditional news media only use Twitter to accumulate followers and online readers and don't respond, interact, or follow readers back. Even worse, some only use the site to post links to their own content, which can be done automatically using sites like Twitterfeed that post the content of RSS feeds into a Twitter feed. This type of one-way communication is the old media way of disseminating news and contradicts the collaborative nature of Twitter. Instead of just posting headlines, the best Twitter feeds are powered by a live human being who selects and posts the most interesting news of the day and retweets and replies to other Twitter users. People are more likely to have an engaging relationship with a human than a robot and Twitter presents an opportunity to infuse personality into news reporting and establish lasting relationships with readers.

Twitter is a great place for discussion about any number of topics, including subjects that are more sensitive than others. As a professional journalist, you should avoid being defensive or attacking other Twitter users. It is okay to disagree, but remember you still represent your newsroom and company. Individual reporters or newsroom staff with their own Twitter accounts should identify themselves by their real name and the name of the company. Twitter profiles can and should include a photo of the journalist or the logo of the news organization and a link to a company website, blog, or individual profile page.

Twitter doesn't have to be all work and no play. Many journalists establish both personal and professional relationships on Twitter and use the site to interact with friends and family as well as sources and other journalists. Some journalists maintain separate personal and professional Twitter accounts. These personal profiles can be set to private so the messages are not seen by the public.

There are many ways to use Twitter, but there is no set style on how you should tweet or what your tweets should include. The best way to attract a significant following on Twitter is to regularly post insightful thoughts and opinions or links to interesting or unique online content. You should develop your own style that works for you and appeals to other Twitter users.

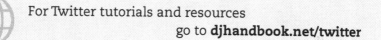

For Twitter tutorials and resources
go to **djhandbook.net/twitter**

Facebook

Facebook (*www.facebook.com*) is a social network with millions of members around the world who use the site to contact new and old friends, share photos, chat online, and send messages to other users. Facebook launched in 2004 as a site for students at Harvard University by then student Mark Zuckerberg. It quickly expanded to other colleges and high schools and later opened its doors to anyone 13-years-old or older with a valid e-mail address.

Each Facebook member creates an online profile where they can post biographical information such as their interests, activities, and contact information. Every Facebook profile page includes a *wall*, a space where friends can post public messages and the user can post links to online articles or content that others can read and comment on. The wall also includes updates of the user's recent activity on the site, including photos they have uploaded or changes made to their profile. Facebook users can keep track of friends by viewing their *news feed*, an area of the site that displays updates about friends' recent activity. Facebook also provides an internal messaging system that functions like e-mail and can be used to send and receive private messages from other users.

One of the first steps to setting up a Facebook account is joining a particular network — either the city or region where you live, the school or university you attend, or the company for which you work. By default, everyone in the same network can view your Facebook profile. For example, if you live in Los Angeles, other Facebook users who also live in Los Angeles will see your profile unless you change Facebook's default privacy settings.

Facebook (www.facebook.com)

Some Facebook members use the site to communicate with family and friends, while many journalists use it as a business tool to share their work, build contacts, and interact with a community of readers. Journalists also use Facebook profiles as a source of information. Some newsmakers and important figures have Facebook profiles that reporters use to gather personal information, identify who they are connected to, or monitor their news feeds for updates.

When someone posts information on a social network like Facebook, they may not intend for it to be seen outside of their friends or family. For example, in 2008, Slate Magazine reported that then 17-year-old Caroline Giuliani, daughter of Republican U.S. presidential candidate Rudy Giuliani, supported rival candidate Barack Obama instead of her father. The information was posted on her Facebook profile and, because it was not set to private, could be viewed by everyone in the same network.

News organizations and other companies are also using Facebook to interact with their audience. Many newsrooms have created Facebook *pages* as a way to connect with users of the site. Pages are similar to normal Facebook profiles, but instead of individuals, pages are dedicated to companies or products. Pages can "friend" other Facebook members, add photos to their profiles, and have walls where other Facebook users can post messages. Facebook users can "Like" their favorite businesses, organizations, and products by subscribing to a page. When a Facebook user becomes a fan of a page, updates or posts created by that page appear in the user's news feed. Many news organizations with Facebook pages use this feature to notify fans of recent news stories or projects or to pose questions to their readers.

A Facebook page

Facebook pages don't have to be created by an actual representative of the organization. For example, the Coca-Cola Facebook page (*www.facebook.com/cocacola*) was created by two Facebook members who really like the brand. The Coca-Cola page has millions of fans and is still maintained by the pair, but they now have the help of the company who provides photos, videos, and other interactive elements.

Facebook pages should actively engage with their community members. The best pages have creative or unique content such as videos and photos and conduct active and ongoing discussions. An effective Facebook page should have a unique and eye-catching profile image, either a logo or an image that represents the organization. This image is one of the first elements of the page that potential fans see. An effective Facebook page should also be updated frequently. You should regularly post new information and media to your page and create and respond to discussion threads and wall posts. Your page should remain active, but be careful not to send too many updates in a short span of time. Facebook users are often more passive compared to users of other social networks and are often annoyed by constant notices, which in turn can cause them to un-"Like" you. Instead, choose the updates that you think are most relevant to your audience.

Facebook users can also create *groups*, which are similar to real-life clubs and can be dedicated to anything from politics to geographic locations and everything in between. Facebook pages are often created and maintained by representatives of a company or organization, but Facebook groups are usually created by individuals. Groups are more likely to focus on a specific interest or issue instead of a brand or company.

Groups are run by "administrators" that manage the group, approve applicants, and invite others to join. They are great for interaction on a smaller scale and are frequently used as a way for members to conduct public discussions or share events with each other. Groups can also be set to private and restrict who can join the group. Newsrooms can create either Facebook pages or groups, but more commonly create pages which are specially designed for companies to interact with Facebook users.

 For examples of Facebook pages and groups created by news media go to **djhandbook.net/newsonfacebook**

A successful Facebook page or group usually requires time before it develops a substantial following. The key to developing an engaging Facebook presence is to share good content and let your readers and your community know about it, even those that aren't already on Facebook. Post links to your Facebook profile or application on your main site and over time your audience and interaction on Facebook will grow.

Digg

Digg (*www.digg.com*) is a social network where members discover and share online articles, photos, and video with other Digg users. Digg is an example of *social bookmarking*, or using the internet to save and share websites and online content with other users. Instead of relying on traditional media to decide what is newsworthy, Digg users collectively determine the popularity of an individual site, story, or article by voting the submission up or down, respectively called "digging" and "burying."

Once online content is submitted to Digg, other users can usually view it in the "upcoming" section of the site. If a submission does not receive enough Diggs, it will eventually disappear from the site's landing pages, decreasing the chance that other Digg users will see or find it on the site. When a submission receives a high number of "diggs," it is promoted to the front page of the site where it is seen by millions of visitors. Many stories are submitted every day,

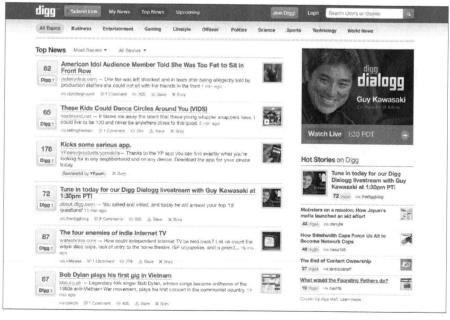

Digg (www.digg.com)

but only the most dugg stories appear on the front page. A site that appears on the front page of Digg can receive hundreds of thousands of visitors in just a few hours. For some smaller sites, the sudden surge of traffic can overload the site and cause it to crash or become temporarily unavailable. The increased traffic — called the "Digg effect" — does not usually last and returns to normal soon after.

Headlines that appear on Digg are often more provocative than traditional news sites or even other social networks because an exciting headline can attract a higher number of diggs. Headlines like "Twitter Banned From White House! Seriously!" or "10 Gadgets We'd Like to Throw into a Black Hole" are not uncommon. Digg users can also replace a story or article's original headline with one they think will attract more diggs. Once a site is submitted to Digg, users can post comments below the headline. Like other social networks, this means whole discussions about a particular news story or article can happen apart from the site where the story originally appeared.

There is a variety of content submitted to Digg, but most submissions are either technology news, offbeat stories, or relate to politics or current events. Journalists can use Digg as a source for story ideas and to find out what is popular or what people are discussing on the web, especially among technology enthusiasts. Journalists and news organizations often look to the site as a tool for self-promotion, but Digg users who only promote their own content are seen as spammers. Before you submit your own content to Digg, you should first build a reputation for finding new and interesting online content from a variety of sources. You should then submit your best content along with your other submissions.

For Digg tutorials and resources
go to **djhandbook.net/digg**

StumbleUpon

StumbleUpon (*www.stumbleupon.com*) is both a social network and search engine where users discover and rate websites, articles, photos, and videos. StumbleUpon is like a personalized recommendation tool for finding interesting content tailored to your interests. Instead of search engines like Google where users look for something specific, StumbleUpon is like channel surfing — you keep clicking a button until you find a website, page, or article that looks interesting. Users can indicate their interests by selecting one or more topics, such as arts, politics, sports, music, and technology. StumbleUpon then presents new and interesting sites based on the user's interests.

StumbleUpon toolbar

StumbleUpon (www.stumbleupon.com)

StumbleUpon users can browse content one of two ways: by clicking a button on the site or by using the StumbleUpon *toolbar*, a row of icons that appears in a web browser after the user installs it. StumbleUpon members can click the "Stumble!" button to find new content and rate any web page by clicking the thumbs up or thumbs down button on the toolbar. The web pages StumbleUpon presents may seem random, but they are based on your interests, how you rated previous pages, and the ratings of other people with similar interests.

Users can submit articles and sites to StumbleUpon by visiting a site or web page and clicking the thumbs-up button. The first person to *stumble* or submit a site is presented with a pop-up window where he or she can submit a review of the site and add a topic and tags that describe the content. Tags are used to categorize a site so it can be presented to others interested in the same topic. Therefore, it is important to select the correct category and include relevant tags. Once a site is indexed and a few people give it a thumbs up, StumbleUpon will show it to many more users. The more thumbs up a site receives, the more users are likely to see it. If a site has already been submitted to StumbleUpon, users can submit a written review of the site by clicking the speech balloon button on the toolbar. Clicking this button also allows you to see users that gave the site or page a thumbs up.

As you rate pages, StumbleUpon will learn over time what you like and match you with similar StumbleUpon users or "stumblers" and show you pages they've given a thumbs up. For example, if you select "journalism" as one of your interests and several other users who also like journalism give an article a thumbs up, StumbleUpon is more likely show you the article because users who matched your interest liked it. StumbleUpon users can subscribe to another user's favorite sites and leave comments on their page. Stumblers can also join groups dedicated to specific topics such as humor, chocolate, or parenting, and share links to related content with other users.

Journalists often focus on Twitter, Facebook, and Digg as a way to build online audiences and direct traffic to their sites, but many news sites receive thousands of visitors from StumbleUpon without ever contributing to or having a presence on the social network. Readers who enjoy a particular story or other content often submit it to StumbleUpon and share it with tens of thousands of like-minded readers who may not otherwise visit the site directly. Twitter and Digg can provide short bursts of increased traffic, but StumbleUpon often creates traffic that lasts long after the content is first published or submitted to the site.

There are a few simple steps to make your content more likely to receive a thumbs up. First, visitors should instantly be able to tell what the story or site is about. Many StumbleUpon users spend just a few seconds or less to determine if the site they are presented is worth exploring further. To attract these users, news sites must incorporate attention-grabbing headlines and keywords, as well as an attractive and eye-catching design in their site to increase the likelihood the casual visitor will spend more than a few seconds viewing the content.

Many journalists are active members of StumbleUpon, though not usually as an official representative of a news organization. Before you submit your own stories or content to StumbleUpon, you should first submit a mix of other interesting sites or you will likely be labeled a spammer. If you submit a variety of interesting articles, others will see you as a great resource. Unlike other social networking sites, you don't want to represent yourself as a business. StumbleUpon reflects the tastes of individuals, not companies or organizations. You should, however, use your real name and/or photo if you use the site to represent a professional news organization.

 For StumbleUpon tutorials and resources
go to **djhandbook.net/stumbleupon**

YouTube

YouTube (*www.youtube.com*) is a video sharing site and social network where users can upload and share videos with a worldwide community of millions of viewers. Anyone can upload a video to the site and comment on other videos that are posted to the site. YouTube began as a destination for wacky videos of everything from cheeky toddlers to homemade music videos. Now, the site is also home to full-length reporting projects from citizen journalists as well as professional news organizations. Citizen journalists are recording and posting video of news events, often armed with just a point-and-shoot camera or a video-enabled cell phone. The type of video that is uploaded to the site is only limited by the imagination and by YouTube's terms of service which bans adult content and copyrighted material that is not property of the uploader.

You don't need an account to watch videos on YouTube, but uploading video to the site requires a free account. Uploading a video is as simple as selecting a file on your computer, adding a title, description, and tags, and posting it to the site. You should always include relevant keywords in your title, description, and tags to ensure that your video appears in the site's search results and is indexed by search engines. Also, the description of your video should be clear and specific. For example, if you upload video of a protest, include a description of when and where the protest happened and what was protested.

A YouTube video

By default, video hosted on YouTube can be embedded on other sites such as blogs and social networks using a unique string of HTML code. The video is still hosted by YouTube, but others are free to embed the video on their site. This feature can be disabled by the uploader if he or she does not want the video distributed on the web.

Every YouTube user who uploads a video automatically creates a video *channel*, a page that contains all the videos they have uploaded, a tally of the number of times each video was viewed, and any comments the user posts on other videos. Channels also display the user's friends and a list of the videos the user has marked as a favorite. You can personalize your channel with information about yourself or organization, as well as upload an image or logo. Many professional news organizations, including *The Associated Press* (youtube.com/AssociatedPress), *The Boston Globe* (youtube.com/thebostonglobe), and Al Jazeera (youtube.com/AlJazeeraEnglish), have launched their own YouTube channels where they share original and previously broadcast content.

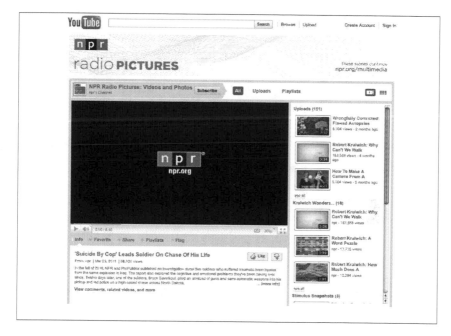

A YouTube channel

News media aren't the only organizations using YouTube channels. The British Monarchy (*youtube.com/TheRoyalChannel*) has posted many official video clips to the social network, including video of royal visits and official ceremonies. The Vatican (*youtube.com/vatican*) has also established an official video channel that features video of various masses and papal visits. Hundreds of news organizations like NPR, CBS, BBC News, and Telemundo have also become YouTube "partners," which means they provide content to YouTube and share in the revenue generated from advertising placed adjacent to their video content.

For a guide to news organizations on YouTube
go to **djhandbook.net/newsonyoutube**

Videographers no longer have to be affiliated with a broadcast news organization to share their work with a worldwide audience. A single video clip posted to YouTube can attract hundreds or even millions of viewers. Many newsrooms post their video stories to their own websites where they are viewed by a substantial number of people, but not even the most popular online news site can compare with YouTube's popularity as a destination for online video. YouTube is one of the most visited sites on the web and the videos posted on the site are viewed millions of times a day by billions of internet users. Many mainstream media outlets have recognized the opportunity to expand their audience and post their video content to both their own site and to video sharing sites like YouTube. By posting video where there are already many viewers, news sites can share their stories with a wider audience than they could by hosting their content solely on their own site. Often, news media drive viewers from YouTube to their websites by including a logo and web address before and/or after each video to indicate where viewers can find more video content. YouTube is the most popular online destination for video, but there are many other video sharing sites with similar features, including Vimeo (*www.vimeo.com*) and blip.tv (*www.blip.tv*). If a video is submitted to YouTube, there are very few reasons why it shouldn't be submitted to other video sharing sites as well.

Most users upload their video to YouTube to share it with as people many as possible. A *viral* video, a video shared rapidly and unexpectedly by many people in a short time, can attract millions of viewers. There is no surefire formula for creating a viral video or driving substantial traffic to YouTube videos, but the most popular videos on the site often contain unique content that is presented in a captivating way. Popular videos are often brief, entertaining, and are created in response to a current event or pressing issue. Journalists, by trade, are already masters of creating this sort of content. YouTube is simply a platform for journalists to share the great content they produce with a larger audience.

 For YouTube tutorials and resources
go to **djhandbook.net/youtube**

Flickr

Flickr (*www.flickr.com*) is both a photo hosting website that contains billions of images uploaded by millions of users and a social network where photographers, both amateur and professional, share and comment on photos posted to the site. Photos of any and everything can be found on Flickr, from photos of news

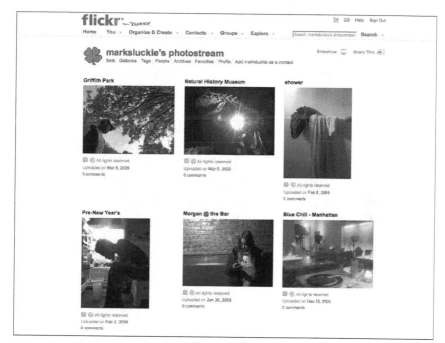

Flickr (www.flickr.com)

and current events to family and vacation photos. After a major news event such as a sporting event or natural disaster, hundreds of photos of the event are usually posted to Flickr by various photographers. Flickr users can also upload and share videos, but photos make up the bulk of the content of the site.

You don't have to be a member of Flickr to view photos posted to the site, but you must have an account to upload or comment on photos. A basic Flickr account is free and users can upload a limited amount of photos each month. A pro account, which can be purchased for a nominal fee, allows the user to upload and store an unlimited number of photos and video.

Both basic and pro Flickr users can organize their photos into *sets*, a group of photos that share a similar subject or theme. Flickr users often add *tags* to their photos and sets to make it more likely that other users will find and view them. Tags are keywords that help other users discover related images and are often the subject of the photo or the location where it was taken. For example, a photo of a band marching in a parade in Los Angeles could be tagged "band," "parade," and "Los Angeles." A Flickr user searching for these keywords is more likely to find the photo.

Flickr is also a social network made up of a community of users who join *groups* centered on specific topics. Flickr groups usually focus on a specific theme, subject, location, or a specific type of camera. Members of a Flickr group can add photos to a photo *pool*, a collection of similarly themed photos taken and submitted by various photographers and can also comment on the submitted photos.

Photographers can also use Flickr as a personal portfolio or as a digital archive for their images. The site is also a great way to showcase your work in a public and easily accessible online space. Flickr users can allow anyone to view or download their photos or change the settings of their account so photos remain private. Like most images that appear on the web, Flickr photos, by default, can be downloaded or saved and are sometimes used without permission on other sites. Some photographers who post their work to Flickr take various security measures to make sure their work is protected, including disabling the download feature and adding watermarks to their images.

Flickr, more than any other social network, represents the divide between traditional and digital media. Many photographers, including professional photojournalists, post their work to the site, but many newsrooms are reluctant to use Flickr for fear their photos will be downloaded and used without permission. Their reservations are not unfounded, but there are some ways newsrooms use Flickr to enhance online photojournalism.

For example, Slate Magazine used Flickr as a tool for readers to submit photos of the recent economic recession to a Flickr pool. Hundreds of submissions were compiled into the project "Shoot the Recession" (*flickr.com/groups/shoottherecession*), which captured various photographers' perspectives on how the economic downturn affected the world around them. The *Walla Walla Union-Bulletin* uses a similar approach and asks users to submit their photos of the southeast Washington city to the Flickr group "Your Walla Walla" (*flickr.com/groups/yourwallawalla*).

Today, ordinary citizens are more likely to carry a camera — either a cell phone camera or a dedicated digital camera — and take photos wherever they go. This means a breaking news event is often photographed by eyewitnesses long before a traditional news reporter arrives at the scene. Journalists can often find photos of a particular event by searching for it on Flickr and can sometimes find a photo that can make or break a story. It can be tempting to immediately download the photo, but as with any other online content, you should first get permission from the photographer before using it on your website or in any other form of publication. Flickr photos remain the property of the photographer even though they are viewable by the public.

Some photos can be used under *Creative Commons* license, a system that allows content creators to share and distribute their work to the public while still retaining the rights to the photo and how it is used. Many Creative Commons-licensed photos are free to use as long as the photographer is given attribution. There are, however, several different levels of restrictions under Creative Commons, including one that indicates that photos are not to be used by for-profit companies which includes most professional news organizations. Be sure to check the type of license associated with a photo before using it. You should also determine whether the photo is property of the person who uploaded it. Some photos may be property of another photographer or a stock photo site. Also, consider whether the photo has been digitally altered or manipulated. To avoid these problems, always use verified and reliable sources.

For Flickr tutorials and resources
go to **djhandbook.net/flickr**

Making the most of social networks

Many news sites establish official profiles on several different social networks, including many of those mentioned in this chapter. These profiles are powered by reporters and editors who interact with their audience and share links to the organization's content. Most social networks require users to identify themselves with a *username*, a unique online alias that can be any combination of letters and numbers (e.g. "washingtonpost," used by *The Washington Post* or "TWCi," used by The Weather Channel). News media who have accounts on several social networks should use the same or a similar username for each account to maintain consistency. In the interest of transparency, journalists should use their real name as their username or identify themselves in their profile with their name and the newsroom they represent. For example, "janesmith" or "JaneSmith_Gazette" is better than "awesomereporter22."

Some social networks like Facebook let members use photos to represent themselves, while others like Twitter require an *avatar*, a photo, graphic, or other image that represents the person or the company.

Many professional news media use the logo of the company, though an avatar can be any image that represents the organization or brand. News organizations should use the same avatar in every official social media profile to maintain a consistent identity across multiple social networks.

Avatars: (from left) CBS News, The (UK) Guardian, The Los Angeles Times,
The Onion, FoxNews.com, The Wall Street Journal

Social networks have become such a common tool among internet users that major news organizations like *The New York Times*, BBC News, and Yahoo! News have hired social media editors and online community managers. These staff members are responsible for developing strategies for how to interact with online audiences and communities using social media. Online news sites also reach out to social network users by including links adjacent to their content that allow users to share what they have read or viewed with others on their social network profiles. These links, usually found at the beginning or end of a news article, can help drive additional visitors back to the news site. Social networks can be used as a tool to increase traffic to a site, but should more importantly be used to enhance online journalism and how the audience interacts with news.

Newsrooms frequently use social networks to post news as soon as it happens instead of waiting hours before the news is announced on-air or published in print. Breaking news can be spread on sites like Twitter within minutes of its occurrence and often while it is still happening, which means mainstream news media no longer have the luxury to wait before publishing news.

Social networks are also used to track the activity of new or existing sources or colleagues. Members of sites like Facebook and MySpace regularly post personal or biographical information in their profiles and contact information such as an e-mail address or physical location. This information can be used by reporters to locate, contact, or find information on a subject of interest when traditional means such as a phone number or home address aren't available. Police and crime reporters, for example, often use social networks to find information on criminals or victims that can be added to a story. The internet has established a new way of finding source material, but also demands a greater responsibility on how journalists distribute it. Information found on social networks can greatly enhance a story, but the person who posted it may never have intended for it to be shared outside of their family and friends. Reporters should also be wary of fake profiles, assumed names, or incorrect information, all of which should be fact-checked and verified before the information is included in a story.

Journalists can also use social networks as a tool for *crowdsourcing*, or gathering information from many people at once to inform or improve a story. For example, journalists often use Twitter to post questions about upcoming stories or to announce to a wide audience that they are looking for more information on a subject or issue. Readers often know more about a topic than an individual journalist, so social networking is a great way to gather this information. Social networks are also a unique way to track reactions to stories. Web users frequently link to, comment on, and discuss news stories with their peers using social media.

Journalists should not sign up for social networks just to promote or improve their own stories. Social networks can transform news into a discussion instead of a one-sided conversation. Depending on your newsroom, you can also use social networks to share upcoming stories and projects or offer a behind-the-scenes look at how a particular story was gathered and reported. Social networks are not the place for boring news writing or to present yourself as a robotic mouthpiece of your newsroom. Instead, be genuine and show your personality, which social networkers appreciate and gravitate toward. Social network users are more likely to establish online relationships with someone who shares a little of themselves with others. Don't just talk to your audience or community — listen and respond to any comments or replies and use social networks as a tool for establishing an open dialogue between the newsroom and the audience.

Journalists aren't just using external social networks to build online communities — some newsrooms have created their own social networks to cater to the specific needs of their readers and viewers. For example, Bakotopia (*www.bakotopia.com*), a project of the *Bakersfield Californian* was launched in 2005 as an online community for the residents of the California city. The site is marketed to young adults who can can create profiles, post personal information and photos, and receive updates on local music and entertainment. The site is so successful that the newspaper launched a companion magazine focused on entertainment and local events. Because there are already so many social networks, those created by media companies must be developed for and marketed to an audience that is underserved. Sites like Twitter, Facebook, and MySpace have cornered the market in global social networking, so it is best to use social media to serve specific communities instead of creating a general interest online destination. Social networks don't have to target a news outlet's entire audience either. A social network can be dedicated to a specific topic such as local politics or nearby restaurants and attract a substantial following.

Journalists themselves are also using social networks to interact with other journalists and for professional development. Specialized social networks for journalists include Wired Journalists (*www.wiredjournalists.com*), which caters to newsroom staff with an interest in digital media, and Visual Journalists (*visualeditors.ning.com*), a site for journalists with an eye for design. Both sites feature even more specific groups like "Blogging" and "Social Bookmarking" for the former and "Page One Design" and "Typography" for the latter. Many journalists are also active on LinkedIn (*www.linkedin.com*), a business-oriented site geared toward professional networking, and Twitter, where journalists frequently discuss ways to better their reporting and improve the industry.

Social networks can be used for both personal and professional reasons. Because of this, many journalists keep their personal profiles separate from their work-related accounts. Many social networks like Twitter and Facebook have privacy settings that let users control who sees the information in their profile or hide the entire profile from public view. Before creating either a personal or professional account, consult your supervisor or your company's policies on social networking to determine if there are any restrictions on what you can and can't include in your profile. For example, many newsrooms restrict employees from sharing internal information or private opinions on social networks. Some companies have explicit policies on what you can and can't share online and some do not allow employees to establish profiles at all. If you do create a profile on a social network, treat everything you post online as public, whether you set your profile to private or not. Be cautious of using social networks to discuss your opinion on a story or subject or to share off-the-record information.

Whether you use social networks for personal or professional reasons, all journalists should join at least one social network. You don't have to join every one listed in this book, only the ones that interest you or can help you interact with your audience. A part of becoming a skilled social network user is remaining active and updating or posting frequently. After some time, you will begin checking your networks with the same frequency as you check your e-mail and posting, tagging, linking, and sharing will become an unshakable habit.

DATA VISUALIZATION

CHAPTER TEN

An important part of a journalist's job is analyzing numbers and trends and turning them into news stories that the reader or viewer can understand. For decades, newsrooms have used *data visualizations* — images or graphics that visually represent numbers, statistics, and other data sets — to uncover patterns and relationships that might otherwise go unnoticed with numbers alone. Columns and rows of data can be overwhelming and hard to navigate and are not the best way to present complex data, either online or in print. Data visualizations help the viewer quickly understand the meaning and connection behind numbers and why they are important.

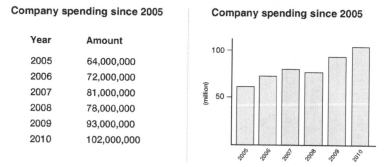

A table that contains information; the same information presented in a visualization

The data visualizations that appear in media publications such as newspapers and magazines are often referred to as *infographics*, a combination of the words "information" and "graphics." Infographics are used not only to represent data and numbers, but also to represent information in a visual way. Infographics are used to make comparisons, show relationships, indicate trends and more. Instead of communicating stories using text, video, or other media that require a considerable amount of time to view or read, infographics can tell a story with a single image. Infographics often focus on a specific set of information and have one clear point. For example, in the graphic above, the chart shows that spending has increased since 2005. Infographics can accompany a traditional text story or can stand alone. *GOOD Magazine* (www.good.is/departments/transparency), for example, regularly publishes infographics that each tell a story or highlight a relevant issue.

There are many ways to visualize data in print and online, including pie charts, bar charts, graphs, and more — examples of which are outlined on the next page. Infographics are especially popular among online audiences with short attention spans because they quickly summarize a story or issue and can be digested in a relatively short amount of time. The internet allows journalists to further improve infographics by adding interactivity and various levels of information to what would otherwise be a flat, unchanging image. Newspapers, for example, only have so much space to accommodate traditional graphics. An online infographic can be searchable, respond to input from the viewer, and include more information in the same space. Maps and databases, two interactive technologies outlined in this chapter, allow the viewer to uncover and explore relevant information and interact with a news story instead of just reading or watching it.

COMMON VISUALIZATIONS

PIE CHART

a circular chart divided into triangular areas proportional to the percentages of the whole

BAR CHART

a chart with rectangular bars with lengths proportional to the values that they represent; used to compare two or more values

LINE CHART

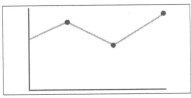

a chart with connecting points that show changes over time

FLOW CHART

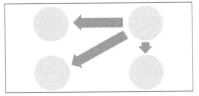

a visual representation of a sequence of events

TIMELINE

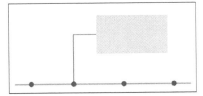

a sequence of related events arranged in chronological order and displayed along a line

WORD CLOUD

a visual representation of the frequency of words that appear in a block of text or speech

HEAT MAP

a visualization that represents values using a color scale

BUBBLE CHART

a chart that presents values as a series of circles

Online maps

Maps are a common type of data visualization used to illustrate information based on a location such as the location of breaking news, local crimes, or places of interest. Online maps are commonly used to plot an address or series of addresses using icons to identify the locations. For example, BBC News (news. bbc.co.uk) often includes a static map of the location of where a story happened adjacent to the story itself.

A BBC News story with an adjacent map

Newsrooms frequently use online maps to visualize crimes committed in a particular area. Crime maps inform readers about the offenses committed in their neighborhood and are an interactive version of the police blotter printed in newspapers. Maps like San Francisco Crimespotting (sanfrancisco. crimespotting.org) include various layers of information in a single interactive map. Users can toggle the map to view the locations of just one type of crime committed in the California city or view all the crimes — including robbery, assault, theft, or arson — at once.

One of the most common ways interactive maps are presented online is using a map mashup. A *mashup* is a web application that combines information from one or more sources and presents it in a new way. A *map mashup* is the combination of location-based data with an online mapping tool like Google Maps, which was originally designed to provide street maps and driving directions. For example, the location of recent traffic accidents can be "mashed up" with a mapping tool and displayed on an interactive map.

San Francisco Crimespotting (sanfrancisco.crimespotting.org)

This form of online mapping is made possible by an API, short for Application Programming Interface, a set of standards for accessing an online application or tool. APIs are accessible to web programmers who can build on the existing services of an online application. For example, the Google Maps API allows anyone to customize and embed Google Maps on their own website or create map mashups. However, you don't have to know how to use an API or how it works to create a map mashup. Third-party tools like Map Builder (www. mapbuilder.net) and UMapper (www.umapper.com) allow anyone to create custom online maps without the technical expertise necessary to use an API. These tools can create custom map mashups that you can embed on your own site or web page.

Most map mashups have similar components and features used to identify locations and add information to the map. On a traditional printed map like the kind you hang on a wall, pushpins are often used to signify a location. The online equivalent of a pushpin is a *marker*, which is used to signify a point on an online map. For example, on a map of a car crash, the marker could be used to point out the location of the collision. Markers used in online maps often look like the silhouette of an ice cream cone, but come in all shapes and sizes.

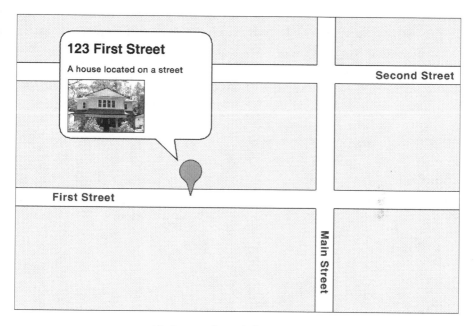

The layout of a typical map mashup

There are several ways to create a marker on a map mashup. Using third-party tools, you can navigate to and click a location on the map, which automatically creates a marker. Alternatively, most mapping tools allow the user to enter an address or intersection and a marker is instantly added to that location. Some locations like bodies of water or unmarked roads have no physical address. These points can be plotted on a map using *latitude* and *longitude* coordinates, a set of numbers that signify a specific location on Earth. Latitude and longitude are imaginary lines that run across the surface of the Earth. The lines of latitude run east and west and longitude runs north and south. The coordinates are obtained by tracing a location on the planet along those lines. For example, New York City's Times Square is located at 40.755971, -73.986702. The first number is the latitude coordinate and the second number is the longitude. You don't have to be a cartographer to determine the coordinates — some online mapping tools, including Map Builder, will automatically calculate the latitude and longitude coordinates if you click a point on the map or search for an address.

Like a pushpin on a printed map, a marker doesn't offer much information about the point other than the location unless information is added to it. On interactive maps, *info windows*, also called *balloons* or *pop-ups*, are used to include a brief description of the marker or its location. When a viewer clicks the marker, an info window that contains information about the marker appears immediately above it. Adding an info window to a marker is like adding a sticky note to a printed map, but instead of just text, the info window can also contain images or even embedded audio or video. With the right mapping tool, an info window can contain any sort of media. However, an info window is usually small and can only contain small amount of information so you should only include at the most a few short paragraphs of text and smaller images or video.

Map makers can also draw lines on their map mashups, similar to drawing on a printed map with a pen or marker. Lines can be used to indicate routes such as the direction of a parade or the path of a police chase.

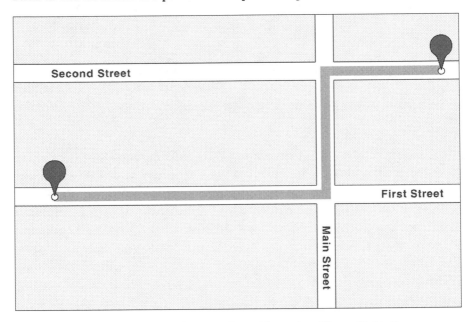

The layout of a typical map mashup with a series of lines added to it

A map mashup can include a single marker or hundreds of markers, depending on the amount of data that is added to it. A flat graphic with too many markers would be crowded, but an interactive map allows users to zoom in on the map to get closer to a specific location, like using a magnifying glass or microscope on a printed map. Online maps with a large number of markers are often accompanied by a list of each marker that appears next to the map. This list makes the map easier to navigate. In some map mashups, clicking any of the points in the list will navigate to that particular marker on the map.

There can often be hundreds or thousands of markers on a single map and plotting and adding information to each one can be a difficult and time-consuming process. Instead of adding markers by hand, some third-party map mashup tools let users upload a CSV file that contains information about each marker. A CSV file (short for Comma Separated Values) is a specially-formatted, plain-text file that stores data or spreadsheet information. A CSV file contains one entry per line (such as an individual marker on the map) and each field in that entry (such as an address or label for each marker) is separated by a comma. CSV files created for online maps often include the name of each location or point, its address, the latitude and longitude coordinates, anecdotal information, or any combination of the above.

Restaurants				
NAME	Lake Café	Mike's Bakery	Moon Diner	Deli Delmonico
ADDRESS	501 E First Street	617 Pine Road	2135 Sea Drive	325 W Third Ave
CITY	Clinton	Fairview	Oxford	Lexington

Information organized in a spreadsheet; a spreadsheet can be converted into a CSV file

Map mashups can be relatively fast and easy to create depending on the amount of points included in the map. Mashups that contain a single point or a few points can be developed quickly and used to illustrate a breaking news story or when there is less time available to create a visual element.

For resources and tutorials on how to create your own online map, go to **djhandbook.net/maps**

Databases

A *database*, a structured collection of information or data, is used to display facts, numbers, statistics, and other information on the web. Instead of using tables or charts to organize information, online news media frequently use databases to present large amounts of information without overwhelming the reader. The main advantage of presenting information in a database is that the online format can contain much more information than can be printed in a newspaper or aired on television or radio. Traditional media often use single incidents to represent a larger issue. For example, the story of a recent car crash could be used to represent a growing number of traffic accidents in an area. Instead of providing a few examples, databases allow readers to see all the numbers or statistics related to a story in one place and draw their own conclusion. Instead of just telling readers that there are, for example, an increased number of traffic accidents in an area, a database can show the number of traffic accidents in the past few years and let readers identify the trend themselves.

You don't have to look far to find source material for a database. Journalists can use the data they already have access to such as arrest records, sports scores, or financial reports. Online databases can take what would otherwise be a complex or inaccessible set of documents and make them accessible and searchable by online readers. For example, The Los Angeles Times' "Homicide Report" (projects.latimes.com/homicide-report/map), a visual database of murder committed in the Southern California area, began as a blog (latimesblogs.latimes. com/homicidereport) with separate posts dedicated to local murders.

The Homicide Report (projects.latimes.com/homicide-report/map)

The Times tapped an existing resource and created a database that lets users view statistics related to area homicides including the location, weapon used, and of the age, race and gender of the victims. While the blog provides anecdotal information, the database provides a historical overview that would otherwise require the viewer to read the entire blog to fully comprehend.

 For examples of online databases created by news organizations, go to **djhandbook.net/newsdatabases**

Creating a well-executed news database requires time, effort, and a considerable amount of technical skill, but is worth the time and effort if it provides a valuable service to readers. Like "The Homicide Report," a good database is useful for months and possibly years after it is first created, especially if it is updated with new information. An active database can be referred to again when the subject of the database is in the news. For example, if *The Los Angeles Times* website runs a story on a local murder, it can include a link back to "The Homicide Report" to explore the topic further.

Databases can be created various ways and take a number of forms, including charts, graphs, and maps. Many online databases include layers of information that are revealed when the user interacts with or clicks links in the database. For example, some databases offer readers the option to sort information by various factors such as date, name, location, or by whatever categories in which the data is arranged. Some databases that contain lots of information also feature a way for readers to search for specific information within that database, often by entering text into a search box or selecting an option from a drop-down menu. For example, Tampa Bay Mug Shots (*mugshots.tampabay.com*), a database of criminals arrested in the Central Florida region, includes a search function that allows visitors to search the index by zip code or by the last name of the person arrested.

Most *dynamic* databases that respond to and display information based on input from the reader are usually backed by complex web programming. There are several programming languages used to create online databases including PHP, MySQL, Ruby, and XML.

XML, short for eXtensible Markup Language, is a computer language used to classify and add context and meaning to data. For example, the sentence "Police arrested David Smith July 14th in New York" has no meaning to a computer. A programmer can use XML to tell the computer that "David Smith" is a person, "July 14th" is a date and "New York" is a city. Structuring information with languages like XML is useful for creating databases in which information is indexed and categorized.

PHP is a scripting language used to build databases, create dynamic and interactive web pages, and store information provided by a user or online visitor. MySQL is a popular database system that allows web applications to store and manipulate data and is often used in combination with PHP. *Ruby* is a web programming language and *Ruby on Rails* is a framework for creating database-driven websites in Ruby. Writing code in a programming language like Ruby takes a lot of time and effort. Rails makes it easier for the programmer to complete common tasks and finish in minutes what would otherwise take hours to do.

These advanced programming languages usually fall outside of the skill set of many journalists, even those who are familiar with basic web development. Before attempting to master any sort of advanced programming, you should first learn and understand computer languages like HTML and how they are used to structure information. Databases can be complex and highly technical, but it is important for reporters and editors to know how online databases work and how they are used to distribute large amounts of information. Some news databases are built by teams of programmers who may or may not be traditional journalists or have formal journalism training, but understand how to visualize data and present it online. Journalists should know enough about database technology to help establish what a database should like, the type of information it should include, and how readers should interact with it. Great databases can take weeks or even months to build, but the hard work that goes into creating them usually results in an invaluable tool for readers.

 For resources and tutorials on how to create a database
go to **djhandbook.net/databases**

Instead of creating a database or visualization for every available data set, some news media are putting raw and unfiltered data in the hands of readers and asking them to discover interesting or newsworthy information within the data or to develop their own visualizations to share with others. A growing number of news media are posting these data sets to their sites, often in downloadable spreadsheets, and allowing readers to explore the information for themselves. For example, *The (UK) Guardian* launched its "Data Store" (*www. guardian.co.uk/data-store*) in 2009 as a destination for data sets on various topics such as school admissions figures and population statistics. Readers are invited to take the data and visualize it any way they choose and post it on their own websites. *The New York Times*' "Visualization Lab" (*vizlab.nytimes.com*) uses a similar approach to data, allowing users to create visual representations of various data sets, including sports stats and standardized test results. The best visualizations are posted on the *Times*' website. These resources empower users to find connections within the data and draw their own conclusions and are another example of using the web as a platform to make journalism a collaborative effort.

For more online data centers maintained by news media go to **djhandbook.net/datacenters**

Creating a visualization

To create a visualization or infographic, you should first select a data set to work with. This collection of information can be anything from a short list of numbers to a complex set of statistics. Journalists have access to or know where to find a variety of data sets, including police records, census figures, test scores, government reports, and other public information that can be used to create a visualization. Once you select your data, you should arrange and format it using a spreadsheet program like Microsoft Excel or a text editing program like Microsoft Word. Sorting your data in a spreadsheet or text document helps organize the information, especially if it is a long list of numbers or statistics. Laying out all your information also makes it easier to identify any trends or patterns within the data.

Sometimes journalists receive paper documents that contain information that is perfect for a visualization, but is not in an electronic format. There are various computer programs that can scan a document and convert into text, but occasionally journalists are required to input the information by hand into an electronic document such as a spreadsheet, especially if it is a smaller amount of information. Data that is transferred manually should be triple-checked for any clerical errors that may in turn cause an error in the visualization. After you arrange and examine your data, you should decide, if not all, what portion of the information is important or can be easily visualized. For example, if your data is a list of the 100 best schools in an area, you may only be able to include the top ten in your visualization so it is simple enough for the viewer to understand.

Data visualization requires an eye for design and the ability to analyze numbers and translate them into an easily understandable graphic or illustration. Online infographics are often created by teams — usually a reporter who organizes the information and identifies the intended message and a news designer or graphic artist who reates a visualization that best illustrates the information.

There are an infinite number of ways to design an infographic or visualization, but many include the same elements. Designers often use proportion to indicate how numbers featured in a graphic are related to each other. For example, to represent 70 percent in a bar chart, the individual bar should take up 70 percent of the total width or height of the graphic, as in the example below. Visual elements that symbolize an exact figure should be carefully designed to accurately represent the number. A visualization that has inaccurate proportions can easily distort the viewer's understanding of the information.

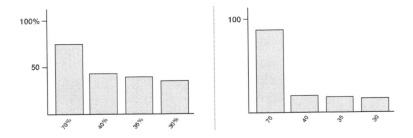

The bar graph on the left has correct proportions; the bar graph on the right does not

Text is usually included in infographics to support the visual elements, but is often not be the main focus of the visualization. Text is often used to label the content of the illustration or is included as a brief description that appears immediately above the graphic. Reducing the amount of text in an infographic will reduce the time required to understand the message or information. The amount of text included in an infographic should also be relative to the size of the graphic. For example, a full-screen interactive infographic can contain much more text than a small web graphic embedded in a web page. Infographics can also use color to focus the viewer's attention on a specific section of the graphic or to guide the viewer's eye through the information. Designers can use all the previously mentioned elements to create a visual message or quickly communicate the importance of the information. Most importantly, the design of the infographic should not be so elaborate that it distracts from the intended message.

Infographics are created using graphic design programs like Adobe Illustrator or Photoshop that can create static graphics for both print and online. The image files can also be transferred to another program like Adobe Flash to add motion or interactivity. Visual journalists can also use programs like After Effects or Maya to create animation or *motion graphics*, moving graphics that play like a video. Some newsrooms take graphics that were designed for print publications, and using one of the previously mentioned tools, make them interactive or add levels of information. The internet presents a unique opportunity to display data in a visual and more interactive way that better informs the audience. Data presented online can and should be better than what would appear in print. Infographics and visualizations should be clear and accurate and the reader should instantly understand what the visual elements represent and, if the data is interactive, how to navigate to find more information. It can be difficult to decide which type of visualization is right to illustrate your information, so let the data or the story behind it dictate the medium in which it is presented.

 For data visualization examples and resources
go to **djhandbook.net/datavis**

FLASH

f

CHAPTER ELEVEN

Flash (*www.adobe.com/products/flash*), a popular piece of software used to create animation and interactive multimedia, was once used solely by animators and graphic artists to create interactive websites and animation. Some time after it was introduced, journalists began using Flash to create multimedia news packages that combine audio, video, images, and/or text. With the increasing use of mobile devices like the iPhone and iPad that cannot display Flash files, the program is being used less frequently in favor of traditional and mobile-friendly web layouts or newer technologies like HTML5. These means of presentation allow viewers to see interactive content on their mobile device. Nevertheless, Flash remains a popular tool for creating interactive infographics, databases, audio slideshows, games, or anything that requires animation or input from the user.

Flash creates a single file that can contain any and all the previously mentioned media and can easily be embedded in a web page. For example, for its multimedia story "Going to the End of the Line" (*http://bit.ly/EndoftheLine*), *The New York Times* created a single Flash presentation that combines photos, audio slideshows, and video to tell the story of the New York City subway system. The online viewer can select a particular train line and view the story for each one without leaving the page.

The New York Times' "Going to the End of the Line," a news story built with Flash

Traditional forms of journalism rely on linear storytelling to communicate a story. A newspaper article, for example, must be read from beginning to end in order for the reader to understand what is written. The reader cannot start reading at any point because the story will likely not make sense. In television and radio, the audience must watch or listen to an entire broadcast to see or hear the news that matters to them — even if it appears near the end of the broadcast. Flash is used to create interactive or non-linear storytelling that allows the viewer to decide what part of the story they want to see or read, stop or start the story at any time, or view sections of the story in any order they wish. For example, "Times of Crisis" (widerimage.reuters.com/timesofcrisis), a project created in Flash, is an interactive examination of the collapse of investment bank Lehman Brothers and the resulting consequences. The story, published by Reuters, includes an interactive timeline that allows the viewer to select a date and discover relevant information that happened on that day. In print, "Times of Crisis" would be one fact after the other, but the Flash presentation allows the viewer to see all or part of the interactive timeline in any order he or she chooses.

Flash can be used to create a whole website or to build animated or interactive

Reuters' *"Times of Crisis"*

elements for a web page. More often, journalists use the program to create multimedia projects that are embedded in a website and displayed online like a photo or video. Flash files are often referred to as movies because they are like little movies that play on the computer. Viewing Flash projects does not usually require any extra steps from the online visitor. Flash Player, the separate but related software that enables web users to view Flash projects online, is, as of this writing, installed on approximately 99% of all web browsers and computers. Those computer users that do not already have Flash Player can download the software from the Adobe website (*get.adobe.com/flashplayer*). Flash files store all the included media elements in a single file and require less time to download compared to the time necessary to download each element separately.

For examples of Flash-based journalism
go to **djhandbook.net/flashjournalism**

The Flash interface

The first step to understanding the possibilities of Flash is understanding the layout and features of the program. The largest area of the Flash interface is the *stage*, a rectangular area in the center of the program where graphics, text, and other visual elements are placed and animation or other effects occur. It is similar to a stage in a theater where actors perform and are visible to the audience. When a Flash movie appears on a website, the viewer only sees the content on the stage. The size of the stage is equal to the size the Flash file will appear on the web. The user can select whatever size works best for the project.

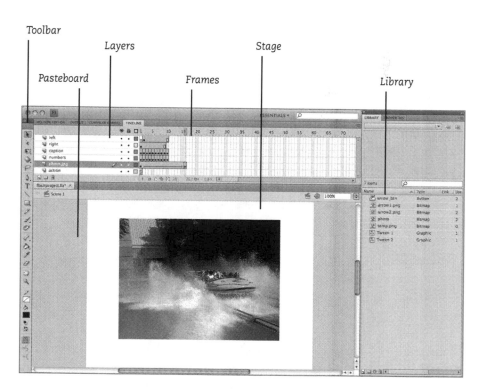

Toolbar — Layers — Stage — Pasteboard — Frames — Library

Flash

The gray area that surrounds the stage is the *pasteboard* and is used for storing elements such as images, graphics, or other media that will not be seen in the final movie. If a Flash project is a theater, the pasteboard is the wings, the area on either side of the stage where actors wait and cannot be viewed by the audience. Any elements or animation that appear on the pasteboard will not appear in the final project.

The *timeline* is an area adjacent to the stage and consists of *layers* and *frames*.

Each frame is a small rectangular box and represents a small stretch of time. For example, if a Flash movie is set to play at 24 frames per second, each frame represents 1/24th of a second. The Flash timeline is like a film strip used in a movie projector. A film strip consists of separate boxes that each represent a frame of the movie and, when run through the projector, creates the illusion of motion.

Frames stretch across the timeline horizontally and together make up layers, which are stacked vertically on the timeline, one on top of the other. Layers are like transparency sheets used on an overhead projector — every layer can be seen unless something is blocking it. An image placed on the topmost layer in Flash will block out an image on the layer below it. Layers can also be rearranged, added, and deleted. Layers are used to organize content that is included in the Flash movie and by default load "bottom-up." This means elements such as images or audio included on the bottommost layer are loaded first. This system allows the viewer begin watching or interacting with the elements on the bottom layers of the Flash movie while the rest of the file continues to download. There are an infinite number of frames and layers in any Flash document, starting at number 1 and going on for as long as you need to create your project.

The red vertical bar that appears on the timeline is the *playhead*. Flash movies are played starting at the leftmost frame and continuing on to the right. The playhead indicates what part of the movie is playing and can be moved manually over a frame to display whatever is on the stage in that particular frame.

Files used in a Flash project are stored in the *library*, which appears on the right side of the Flash interface. The library is a list of elements that are created in or imported into Flash such as graphics, audio files, and video clips. Elements stored in the library can be retrieved and reused as many times as necessary. The more complex the Flash project, the more elements the library contains.

The *property inspector* — which appears on a tab next to the library or, in older versions of the program, at the bottom of the Flash interface — displays information about specific elements in the Flash project and changes depending on the element selected. For example, when the user selects the stage, the property inspector shows information about the stage such as the size of the Flash project and the background color. When a specific element on the stage is selected, the property inspector displays the object's width and height, the type of element it is, and its location on the stage. The property inspector also allows you to change the previously mentioned characteristics of Flash elements.

The *toolbar*, a vertical row of icons to the left of the stage, contains drawing tools that are used to create rectangles, lines, and circles as well as tools for selecting elements on the stage. Flash can be used to draw animation and graphics from scratch, though tools like Photoshop and Illustrator, also distributed by Adobe, offer greater flexibility.

For step-by-step tutorials on how to use Flash
go to **djhandbook.net/flash**

The capabilities of Flash

All Flash projects, even the most complex ones, are based on the same core principles and include many of the same elements. Text is a common element included in Flash projects, especially for news or multimedia packages. Text in Flash can be formatted just like the text in a word processing program like Microsoft Word. Flash users can change colors, fonts, and text alignment and can even create links to other websites. Text can also be animated, but in professional projects, animated text should be kept to a minimum so as not to annoy the viewer with unnecessarily moving objects.

There are three types of text used in Flash: static, input, and dynamic. *Static text* is used for headlines, captions, or other text that does not respond to input from the user. *Input text* is used to obtain information from the user and is commonly used to create forms. The input text feature in Flash creates a field where the user can type in text. The third type of text is *dynamic text* and is used in combination with programming languages to change the text included in a Flash movie or to load text from outside of the program. Text included in Flash should be limited to a few paragraphs or less because the program was not designed to display large blocks of text. Text displayed in Flash is noticeably less clear and less readable than text displayed on a normal web page.

Flash is best used for displaying or animating images, graphics, or photos. Various image formats, including JPG, PNG, and GIF, can be uploaded into the program (see Chapter 4 for a description of these image types). Photos and images should be edited and resized before they are imported into Flash, because the program has no photo editing capabilities.

Journalists also use Flash to create animation and effects that visually enhance a multimedia project. Flash users can move, resize, rotate, morph, and alter the transparency of any of the elements included in a Flash project. This basic animation is often generated using a process called *tweening*, or changing the position or shape of an object. To create a tween, you must first create the first and last frames of the animation. Flash fills in the missing information and creates the appearance of movement.

For example, to make a photo move from left to right across the stage, place the photo on the left side of the stage in the frame and on the right side of the stage in another frame. When you create the tween, Flash fills in the blanks to make the photo appear as if it is moving across the screen. Tweens are created using *keyframes* or single frames that indicate where a major change takes place in the Flash movie. Instead of creating individual frames for each bit of animation — for example, placing the photo at various points across the stage until it reaches its destination — the user can tell Flash to start at one keyframe (in this case, the leftmost photo) and end at another keyframe.

An illustration of a tween; the photo moves from left to right

Flash, as mentioned previously, can be used to create interactive stories that respond to input from the viewer. Interactivity in Flash is created using *actions*, bits of code that instruct Flash to perform various tasks in the movie. Actions are created using *ActionScript*, the scripting language that powers Flash. ActionScript can create actions that are as simple as starting a video when a button is pressed or can create complex interactive games and databases. ActionScript is frequently used to create interactive *buttons* that, when clicked, direct the viewer to different parts of the Flash movie, open a web page or site, or start or stop a function of the movie. Buttons can be text, images, or graphics and, like hyperlinks that appear on the web, are commonly used for navigation. For example, many Flash projects produced by news organizations contain multiple interviews or profiles that are divided into separate sections in the Flash project. The viewer can see each interview by clicking on a button, often a picture or the name of the interviewee. This technique is used in the "Going to the End of the Line" multimedia story. By clicking on each photo or train line, the viewer is taken to a different photo slideshow or video within the same Flash project.

ActionScript is similar to computer languages like HTML or CSS, but has its own elements unique and structure. For example, the basic ActionScript code below, if added to a button, tells Flash to go to the 33rd frame of the movie when the user clicks the button.

```
on (press){
gotoAndPlay(33);
}
```

ActionScript can quickly become very complex so the easiest way to learn the language is to master the basics and learn the rest on a project-by-project basis. Think of the specific functions you want for a particular project and, using an ActionScript book or a search engine like Google, locate a tutorial that contains instructions on how to create that function. For example, if you want to create interactive buttons for your project, find a tutorial that specifically addresses interactive buttons. Over time, you will become familiar with the ins and outs of the scripting language. For those with no web development experience or who just need a little guidance, Flash comes with "Script Assist" mode which helps novice users create common ActionScript functions and eliminates the need to write code from scratch.

For Flash and ActionScript resources and tutorials
go to **djhandbook.net/flash**

Aside from images and text, one of the most common media included in Flash journalism projects is audio. Audio can be used to play clips of interviews or can be paired with photos to create audio slideshows. Flash users can import several types of audio files into the program, including MP3, WAV, and AIFF files (see Chapter 5 for a description of these audio files). All audio should be edited before it is imported into the program. Flash has a built-in sound editor, but a dedicated audio editing program offers greater flexibility and control over the sound. Flash can also be used to add special audio effects that are synchronized with animation or play when the user clicks a button, but these effects should be limited in professional news projects. Including unnecessary audio files can increase the size and the time required to load the project and can also distract from the content. If you include audio in your Flash project, you should indicate to the viewer that there is audio present and also include a way to turn it off. Some online visitors may view a Flash project in a quiet area and an unexpected blast of sound may send the viewer scrambling for the volume button.

Flash producers can also include video in their Flash projects, either as part of a multimedia package or as a standalone video player. Several video file types, including MOV, AVI, and MPEG, can be imported into Flash (see Chapter 7 for a description of these video formats). Like audio, video should be edited before it is imported into the program.

The interactive buttons that control the behavior of a Flash movie make the program ideal for creating an embeddable audio or video player. Flash allows the user to add custom playback controls to a video or audio file such as the ability to play, stop, fast forward, rewind, and control the volume, and can even include a scrubber and progress bar. The video or audio player can then be embedded in a web page. Because Flash is already installed on most computers, many popular media-sharing sites, including YouTube, use Flash to make video files available on the web. Flash media players can also be designed to play multiple files in a single player.

Because of their size, video and audio files can dramatically increase the file size of the Flash movie and the time required to load and view the file. Online viewers are notoriously impatient, especially when it comes to loading Flash files, and may click away without waiting for the project to load and never see the contents of the movie. If video or audio files longer than a few seconds are included in a Flash movie, the Flash file should also include a *preloader*, a visual indicator that informs the viewer that the content in the Flash project is loading. A preloader loads the media contained in the Flash file before the movie starts so, instead of staring at a blank screen, visitors are presented with a visual element that indicates exactly how long it will take the project to load. Preloaders come in many shapes and forms, but are often a rectangular progress bar or percentage indicator that counts down the time until the Flash file is ready and all the files are loaded. After the project is loaded, the Flash movie begins. A preloader increases the probability that a visitor will wait while the project loads, but only if that wait time is relatively short.

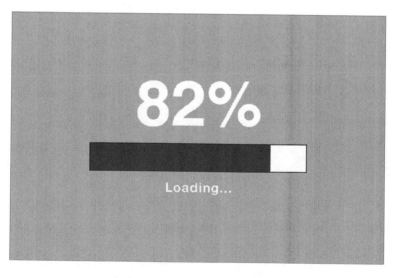

The layout of a typical Flash preloader

If a project takes a while to load, even with a preloader, bulky files like audio and video should be loaded *externally* using ActionScript. This is done by uploading the files to a web server and, using some basic coding, indicating to Flash where to find and retrieve the files. Loading media externally decreases the size of a Flash file and reduces the time necessary to load a project.

For resources and tutorials on how to create a preloader
go to **djhandbook.net/preloaders**

Slideshows, a common form of online presentation in which a series of photos with a similar theme or subject are displayed in sequence, can be built with Flash. The program was originally used to create animation and can easily handle transitions such as fades and dissolves. Because Flash files can also include audio, you can use the tool to build *audio slideshows* that display photos and play audio at the same time. You can also create short blocks of text to display captions and even include several slideshows in a single Flash file. Soundslides, a program outlined in Chapter 6 that is used to build Flash-based slideshows, is great for creating slideshows without knowing Flash. However, building photo or audio slideshows in Flash gives the user more flexibility and every detail — from the timing to the design to the navigation — can be controlled by the producer. A slideshow created in Flash can also be built to a specific size or incorporate a color scheme or design that mirrors the website where it is posted.

For examples of slideshows created with Flash
go to **djhandbook.net/flashslideshows**

Infographics, short for information graphics, have long been used in print journalism to visually illustrate complex statistics or data. Flash can enhance charts and diagrams by making them animated or interactive. Flash is also used to add navigation and layers to include more information in one space than could fit in a traditional print graphic. *USA Today* (*www.usatoday.com*), a publication known for its eye-catching print infographics, brings the same eye for visual journalism to its online interactive graphics. The site adds a level of interactivity to its online content that is not possible with print graphics. For example, to illustrate the features of the Dallas Cowboys stadium in Texas, *USA Today* created a Flash infographic (*http://bit.ly/Cowboys-Stadium*) that lets the viewer explore the stadium using interactive navigation. The Flash project reveals various levels of information such as the design of the structure and a comparative illustration of the size of the stadium, all of which is included in a single Flash file.

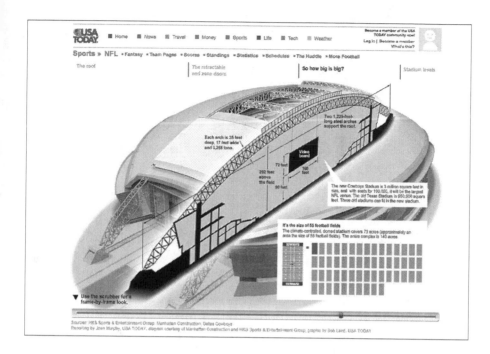

USA Today's "Inside Cowboys Stadium," an interactive infographic built with Flash

For more infographics built with Flash
go to **djhandbook.net/flashgraphics**

Before journalists began using Flash, the program was — and still is — used to build interactive games that respond to input from the player. Flash games combine graphics, sound, and animation and can be simple or very complex. News organizations often create Flash games that are both educational and entertaining. For example, Swarm Interactive (*www.swarm.md/interactive_portfolio. html*), an interactive design firm that creates unique content for online media like Discovery Channel and *National Geographic*, develops games that teach players complicated subjects in a simple and fun way. For example, in the interactive game "Volcano Explorer," users can toggle various levels to create a virtual volcano. The game was built and animated with Flash.

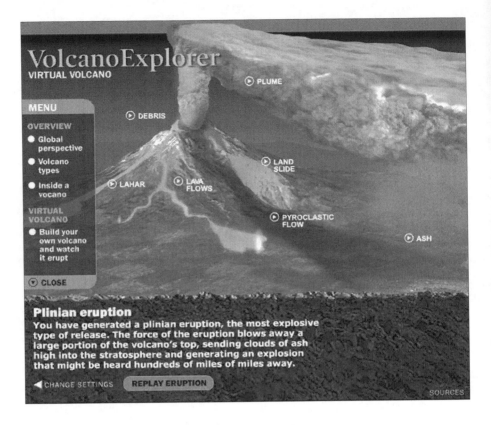

"Volcano Explorer," a Flash game

Flash games are powered by lots of ActionScript and can take a substantial amount of time to create. Because of their complexity, Flash games that appear on online news sites are often built by dedicated Flash programmers with experience creating complex Flash projects.

A subset of the Flash game is the Flash quiz, which is often much more simple to create and for the user to play. Flash can be used to build several types of input forms such as multiple-choice or fill-in-the-blank which, when paired with questions, creates interactive quizzes. Flash can also be used to develop match games where players drag images to their correct location using interactive buttons. Flash quizzes can be customized to record the player's answers and produce a score. Many of the quizzes found on People.com (*games.people.com/games.trivia*), including multiple choice and interactive quizzes that test readers' knowledge of celebrities, are built in Flash.

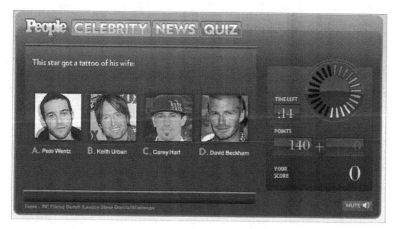

People.com's "Celebrity News Quiz"

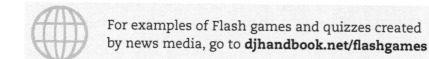

For examples of Flash games and quizzes created by news media, go to **djhandbook.net/flashgames**

Flash can also be used to build online databases that store and display large amounts of data, numbers, and statistics and incorporate common features found in databases such as search tools and interactivity. Flash databases can be either static or dynamic. To create a static database, data is imported or copied and pasted into Flash and is styled or made interactive, but the content doesn't change unless the actual Flash file is changed. Dynamic Flash databases are paired with computer languages such as ActionScript, XML, or PHP to import external text or data into the Flash project. Developing dynamic databases means the content can be changed outside of Flash without actually changing the Flash file and is useful for adding or substituting new information in an existing file. Dynamic databases can also be customized to display information based on input from the viewer.

For examples of databases built with Flash
go to **djhandbook.net/flashdatabases**

When you design a Flash project, it is important that you do not ignore the conventional rules of web design. Multimedia projects designed in Flash can be built from scratch and can be as creative as you want. It can be tempting to make everything in your project move, swish, zoom, or fly across the screen. However, you shouldn't build or add elements just because they look "cool" or make Flash projects so complicated that the viewer doesn't know how to use it. Flash projects should mimic regular websites by providing navigation that is easy for the audience to use and a layout that presents the information as simply as possible. Flash is used to enhance news stories and the design of the project should support, not distract from the content.

Multiple Flash projects posted to a single site should be visually consistent. In most cases, the colors, fonts, and layout used in the Flash file should fit in with the rest of the site where the project is published. Many newsrooms have set sizes for their Flash projects and specific guidelines for where design elements such as headlines and captions should be placed. To save time, create templates for your Flash files that can be used repeatedly and reduce the need to build everything from scratch for every project.

Publishing Flash files

When you create a project with the Flash program, all the elements created or imported in the project, including images, frames, and tweens, are saved in an FLA file. Media files such as photos and audio clips that are imported into a project are saved and stored in the FLA file and do not have to be uploaded again. However, to display a Flash file on the web you must create a SWF file. SWF (pronounced "swiff") is the version of the Flash movie that is embedded on a web page. When a Flash project is "published," the program converts all the files and animation included in the FLA into a SWF file that contains only the information needed to play the Flash movie. A SWF file is considered the finished project and cannot be edited. If you want to make changes to your FLA movie, you must open the original FLA file in the program and create a new SWF file.

In addition to creating the SWF, publishing a Flash file also creates an HTML file that contains the code you need to embed the SWF into a web page. Every HTML file created by Flash contains code that tells the browser how to display the Flash movie.

To post your project to the web, upload the SWF file and, optionally, the HTML file to the location on the web server where it will reside. If you use a content management system, you are often required to upload only the SWF file. To embed a Flash file in a CMS, copy and paste the HTML code created by Flash into the appropriate field in the CMS. You must remove a few lines from the code created by Flash and include the complete web address of the SWF file:

```
<object classid="clsid:d27cdb6e-ae6d-11cf-96b8-444553540000"
codebase="http://download.macromedia.com/pub/shockwave/cabs/
flash/swflash.cab#version=10,0,0,0" width="600" height="800"
id="myflash" align="middle"><param name="allowScriptAccess"
value="sameDomain" />
<param name="allowFullScreen" value="false" />
<param name="movie" value="myflash.swf" /><param
name="quality" value="high" /><param name="bgcolor"
value="#828282" /><embed src="http://www.mysite.
com/myflash.swf" quality="high" bgcolor="#ffffff"
width="600" height="800" name="myflash" align="middle"
allowScriptAccess="sameDomain" allowFullScreen="false"
type="application/x-shockwave-flash" pluginspage="http://www.
adobe.com/go/getflashplayer" />
</object>
```

The disadvantages of Flash

Flash is a unique program and its uses are only limited to the imagination, but the program does have its disadvantages. Designing a project in Flash means the viewer can't bookmark or link to a specific point in the project like they would on a normal web page. This is because all the information in Flash is contained in one embedded file. Some newsrooms have worked around this problem by breaking one Flash story into several individual files. This way, each part of the Flash story can be posted to its own web page that can be easily bookmarked. If Flash files are separated this way, each file should have the same navigation system and design. Also, until recently, the content of Flash files was not indexed by search engines, which presented a problem for many newsrooms who wanted to drive traffic to their Flash projects. Now, sites like Google can index the text included in online Flash files and present it in search results.

Flash has become such a popular tool in the journalism industry that many news organizations use the program when another medium such as video, audio, or even flat graphics would be more appropriate. Before designing a multimedia project in Flash, decide if Flash is the best way to tell the story or if it can be told using other technology. Often, a simple web page with embedded images, audio, or video is easier to construct than building the same project in Flash. Use the program to add elements to a story that can't be created using other technology such as interactive and non-linear storytelling.

Most importantly, unlike other digital technologies such as video and audio, there is a steep learning curve that the beginning user must conquer to produce the amazing things Flash is capable of creating. Most of the outstanding multimedia and interactive Flash projects featured on news sites are created by dedicated Flash developers with years of experience. Even with training, it takes a considerable amount of time to build even the most basic Flash projects. With a print story, the writer can wrap up their thoughts and simply stop writing if a deadline is approaching. This is not always possible with Flash. Everything must work properly, the code must be complete, and every hole must be closed, which means a Flash project is only finished when it is absolutely done. You can reduce some of the time required to build Flash projects by removing unnecessary elements or animations that make the project more complex, but in general Flash projects still take a considerable amount of time to build.

Flash producers should develop templates that can be reused for multiple projects and reduce the time necessary to build frequently used elements such as buttons, navigation, and captions. Templates can also be created for Flash slideshows for which the producer only has to replace the photos and text for each new slideshow. Templates also ensure that Flash projects that appear on a site have the same layout and design.

Building projects in Flash requires the visual mind of a designer, the technical mind of a computer programmer, and the storytelling skills of a journalist. The Flash producer must design the layout of the project and how the user will interact with it, much in the same way a web developer creates a website. Because Flash requires many different skills, Flash projects can and should be created collaboratively. One person can be responsible for storyboarding the project, another can design the layout, and someone else can code or build the actual Flash file. This sort of collaboration is, after all, one of the hallmarks of digital journalism.

WHAT NOW?

?

CHAPTER TWELVE

If you read this book from cover to cover or even if you just read the table of contents, you've probably realized that there are many tools used for digital journalism and that learning them all could take a very long time. You don't have to know the ins and outs of every tool or piece of equipment, but you should be aware of how they work, their capabilities, and how they contribute to digital storytelling. Once you are aware of the various tools used to present journalism online, identify the tools you are interested in and you'd like to master or learn more about. If you start learning a skill that you are comfortable with or that excites you, you have a far greater chance of mastering it than you would by attempting to learn everything at once. Also, some skills are based on similar principles and if you learn one technology, you can sometimes just as easily learn a related technology. For example, if you master the basics of still photography, you will have an easier time learning video which is based on many of the same techniques and guidelines.

A person who is a master of all the tools featured in this book is rare. Though these jacks-of-all-trade do exist, more often journalists are experienced in one or a few areas of digital journalism and work collaboratively with a team of other journalists to produce multimedia or interactive stories. Smaller newsrooms often have a single person or a small group of producers who create multimedia content for the publication. Larger newsrooms are more likely to have groups of staff that are each dedicated to a particular area of multimedia. For example, in larger newsrooms, one or more reporters record and edit video, another person or group shoots photos, and another group is responsible for audio gathering and editing. In both types of newsrooms, everyone works together to produce journalism that communicates a story, no matter the medium.

If you are just starting out in digital journalism, experiment with basic equipment and learn its core functions and features before moving on to more advanced tools. For example, novice photographers should practice with point-and-shoot cameras and audio producers should gather sound with a basic, but professional digital audio recorder. Also, before investing lots of money in pricey computer programs used to produce digital journalism, consider using software for a trial period to learn how it works and determine whether you can eventually master the program. Many of the computer programs mentioned in this book, including Flash and Soundslides, allow anyone to use the program on a trial basis before actually purchasing it. Software distributor Adobe (*www.adobe.com*), for example lets anyone try many of its programs free for 30 days, including Flash, Photoshop, Dreamweaver, and several other tools used for multimedia production. There are also free online alternatives to some popular programs, many of which have the same functions as their pricier counterparts. If you find that you are not skilled at using a particular tool you can move on to something else and not feel tied to an investment.

 For a guide to free alternatives to popular multimedia programs, go to **djhandbook.net/free**

The quickest way to learn digital journalism tools is to practice frequently, both in and out of the newsroom. Shoot photos wherever you go or start producing your own video projects in your spare time. The more you use these tools, the more familiar you will become with them and you will eventually spend less time building your digital media stories when you are in the newsroom. Once you become comfortable with the equipment or software of your choice and begin to produce content that you are proud of, ask your friends or colleagues to review your work and give you feedback. Ask them what they did or didn't like about what you created and if there are any areas where you can improve. Having a small audience view your work will help you develop your skills before you publish it to a worldwide audience. If you prefer to learn in a classroom setting, several organizations such as the Poynter Institute (*www.poynter.org*) and the Knight Digital Media Center (*www.knightdigitalmediacenter.org*) conduct workshops that train journalists to use various digital media tools. Similar workshops are taught around the world by various journalism and independent groups. For more online resources and do-it-yourself training, consult the many tutorials available at the links listed in this book or follow the link below.

For a guide to online tutorials and resources for multimedia training, go to **djhandbook.net/training**

Part of becoming a digital journalist is not only knowing how to use digital media tools, but also how to think like a digital journalist. The new era of journalism requires reporters and editors to be familiar with multimedia, interactive, and non-linear forms of storytelling. Digital journalists must also have the wisdom to decide which of all the tools available is right for a particular story. Visual stories are best told using photos or video and stories with great sound are best told using audio, but along with these elements are a variety of ways to present them on the web such as audio slideshows, multimedia packages, or standalone media players.

Digital journalists often think of original and creative ways to share stories and how to make them interesting and engaging for the reader or viewer. For example, there are hundreds, if not thousands, of audio slideshows on the web. Skilled digital journalists know how to combine the elements of a slideshow into a compelling presentation that captures the essence of the story and stands out from the thousands of other slideshows. The best digital journalists are mavericks and risk-takers who the journalism community appreciates for being the first to try something new. On the other hand, digital journalists should not use technology just for the sake of creating something "cool" and should strive to use digital tools to enhance, not distract from the story. Journalists should also have the wisdom to understand when to create an elaborate multimedia project and when to use simple text or photos to tell a story.

There are a great number of news media who are producing exceptional multimedia content and to whom other news organizations look to for inspiration for their own work. It is okay to draw inspiration from the unique content produced by large publications like *The New York Times* that often have greater resources than the average newsroom. However, you should also look outside of journalism to see how other industries are using digital tools to enhance their work. Multimedia production isn't limited to just news media: many other fields from education to architecture to the creative arts are also using multimedia tools to present information both on and offline.

For both aspiring and veteran journalists, it doesn't matter if you master every digital media tool in this book if no one sees your work or knows who you are. In the digital age, journalists are no longer faceless entities of the companies they work for. Journalists are using the web and social networks to promote their work and to establish personal and professional relationships outside of the newsroom. Every digital journalist should share their talent and market themselves by creating an online portfolio of their work. An online portfolio can include examples of stories, photos, audio, video, and other media that the journalist has produced. An online portfolio is often a better representation of your skills than a traditional résumé and can also include a blog to provide recent updates about your work. Your portfolio should also include a downloadable résumé, contact information, and, optionally, a photo of yourself. A portfolio doesn't have to be fancy, but it should showcase your personality and demonstrate what sets you apart from others.

Younger journalists do not have to wait until their stories are published in a print publication to start writing or work at a broadcast station to produce television or radio pieces to include in their résumé or portfolio. The internet is an excellent platform for publishing a body of work and obtaining the experience that many news media require new hires to have. There are fewer internship opportunities than there were years ago which means the chance that a student will gain experience in a professional newsroom is less likely. Aspiring journalists can create and post content to blogs, vlogs, video channels, podcasts and more to establish their talent without waiting for a news organization to provide them a forum to do so. Posting original content to the web without prompt also demonstrates a commitment to creating quality journalism.

Journalists, both employed and unemployed, are now their own brands and can establish a name for themselves as an authority for news in their beats. Many journalists who have full or part-time jobs also develop independent projects outside of the newsroom that range from personal blogs to books to online resources. You may have to consult with your supervisor for permission to produce content not related to your position, but doing so offers you the opportunity to develop projects that interest you, but that you may not be able to work on during your day job.

If you do choose to create your own online site or even if you just participate in any of the various social networks or online forums, be very conscious of the *digital footprint* you leave behind. Today, finding out about a person, their background, and even their contact information is as easy as entering their name into a search engine like Google. Using a search engine, anyone can track down your online activity, including social network profiles, blogs, comments made on websites, articles written by or about you, and any other personal information. Online content can be accessed and read days, months, or even years after it is first published unless it is actively deleted. Current or potential employers or even curious readers or viewers can quickly find anything negative or potentially controversial posted to the web, which can in turn damage your reputation or credibility. This can be especially troublesome for aspiring journalists. Employers often search for candidates' online activity in addition to scanning a traditional résumé. If you have naughty photos on Facebook or other potentially damaging information posted on the web, remove it before someone else finds it. Make sure everything you post online is something you wouldn't mind the world seeing.

In addition to an acceptable online profile, college and university students should aim to graduate with a diverse set of technical skills. It is no longer enough to be experienced in one area of journalism such as print or broadcast. To compete with thousands of other grads as well as other job-seeking journalists, you must have a range of digital media skills that separate you from your colleagues. The more digital tools you learn, the more you establish yourself as a journalist who can thrive in today's modern newsroom. The same advice applies to veteran journalists who, if they do not show they are capable of presenting stories in more than one medium, are at risk of losing their jobs. Journalists should not only learn digital media tools to stay competitive, but also to provide a better experience for their readers or audience.

Aim to master — or at least speak knowledgeably about — as many technologies as possible, starting with the ones outlined is this book, but remember this is only the starting point. Journalism and its associated technologies are changing at a rapid pace and if you don't continually update and freshen your skills, you'll find that they will become obsolete. As cutting-edge as some of the technologies featured in this book are, the unfortunate truth is that many will be obsolete in just a few years. Newer technologies like mobile websites and applications are already standard in many newsrooms and each journalist must know what is possible with these technologies. To thrive in this industry means to evolve along with it. Be aware of existing and upcoming technology and how it can be applied to journalism. If you are always at the forefront of online journalism, you will never be left behind.

Even with all the technology that is transforming the industry, there is still is a need for hardcore journalism — the kind that exposes the corrupt and champions the downtrodden. The medium in which the news is published may change but the values of journalism — fair and accurate reporting, credibility, and the search for truth — will never go out of style. All the tips and tricks included in this book aren't the answer to saving journalism, but they are the tools that today's tech-savvy readers use to consume and share news. No one is sure what the future of journalism will look like, so journalists should take advantage of every available opportunity and tool to share news with readers, viewers, and listeners. Despite the doubtful outlook for many media companies and newsroom, journalism will exist in some form or another. You've made it to the end of this book which shows that you and other journalists like you have the power to transform the industry and the future of news.

GLOSSARY

A

ActionScript
programming language used to control and add interactivity to Flash movies

aiff
Audio Interface File Format; an uncompressed digital audio format developed by Apple

ambient sound
sound that naturally occurs at a scene, used in audio editing to establish location or create a sense of environment; also *natural sound, nat sound* or background noise

analytics
a program or online tool that gathers data about how a website is accessed, used to study the behavior of website visitors

API
application programming interface; a set of standards for accessing an online application or tool often used by developers to expand the services of an existing online program

autofocus
a feature on digital cameras that analyzes the distance from the camera to the selected subject and automatically adjusts the focus

avatar
a photo, graphic, or other image used to represent a web user's online identity, often used in social networks and forums

AVI
Audio Video Interleave; a compressed video file format developed by Microsoft

B

b-roll
supplemental video or audio footage that supports or illustrates the main story

backpack journalist
a mobile journalist whose digital media tools, such as a video camera, audio recorder, or laptop, fit into a backpack

blog
an online journal that displays entries in reverse chronological order; to write in this style

blogosphere
the collective online community of bloggers and their blogs

browser
computer software used to access and navigate the web

C

cardioid
the heart-shaped sound pickup pattern of a unidirectional microphone

CCD
charge coupled device; an electronic sensor that converts light entering a camera lens into electrical signals

citizen journalist
a person without professional journalism training who disseminates news and information, often using the internet to do so

CMS
see *content management system*

code
the characters and terms that make up a computer language; to add computer language to text; to program a website or computer application using a computer language

color temperature
a measurement of color expressed in degrees Kelvin

compression
a technique used to reduce the size of a file or data

content management system (CMS)
an online tool or computer software used to create, publish, edit, and manage the content of a website

convergence
the combination of one or more forms of journalism

Creative Commons
a license that allows content creators to govern how their work is used; the non-profit organization that establishes such licenses

crowdsource
to use the internet as a means for gathering information from a large group of online users

CSS
Cascading Style Sheets; a programming language used to style a website or page

CSV
Comma Separated Values; a plain text file that stores data separated by commas

D

data visualization
the use of images or graphics to represent numbers, statistics, or information

database
a structured collection of online records or data

Delicious
a social network where users store, share, and discover links to online content

developer
in computing, a person who creates and/or designs software or applications

Digg
a social network where users discover and share articles, photos and video

digital footprint
evidence of a computer user's online activity, including information posted to social networks or blogs

Django
a web framework based on the Python programming language used to build complex web applications

Dreamweaver
web design software used to create online content

Drupal
an open source content management system

DSLR
Digital Single Lens Reflex; a digital camera in which the scene is viewed through the same lens that takes the photo

dynamic
in web design, a website or page that changes based on user interaction

E

embed
in web design, to include an element, such as a video or audio player, on a web page

F

Facebook
an online social network where members connect with friends, share photos, chat online, and send messages

FireWire
a system for connecting a computer to external electronic equipment; a type of cable used to transfer information to and from a computer

flame war
a hostile argument between two or more users in an online forum or message board

Flash
software used to create animation, multimedia, and interactive stories

Flickr
an image and video hosting website and online social network

focus
a camera feature that controls the sharpness of an image; to use said feature

forum
an online discussion site

FTP
File Transfer Protocol; a method used to transfer files from one computer to another

G

geotagging
the process of adding geographical data to various media such as photographs or web pages

GIF
Graphics Interchange Format; a digital image format that displays up to 256 distinct colors

grayscale
a photo or digital image that consists only of varying tones of black and white

H

head room
in video and photography, the space between the top of the subject's head and the top of the frame

HTML
Hypertext Markup Language; the computer language used to create pages and content on the Web

hyperlink
on the web, a word or phrase that, when clicked, takes the user from one web page to another; to create or enable such links

hyperlocal journalism
journalism that focuses on or caters to a relatively small area, city, or neighborhood

I

infographic
a visual representation of information or data; short for "information graphic"

interactivity
in journalism, a term that describes online content that responds to input from the user

interface
the arrangement and components of a computer or web application
with which the user interacts

J

JPG
Joint Photographic Experts Group; a digital image file that can display
up to 16 million different colors

K

keyword
a word or phrase that is significant or relevant to the topic of an
article, story, or other online content

L

lavalier
a small microphone usually worn on the body

LCD
liquid crystal display; a flat screen used to view images on digital
devices such as photo and video cameras

lead room
the space in front of and in the direction of the subject; also *nose room*

link
see *hyperlink*

link journalism
the curation of relevant internet links to form a single story

linkblog
a blog that consists of links to other content

LinkedIn
a business-oriented social networking site

liveblog
a blog or site that is updated in real-time during a particular event

lower third
text that appears in the lower portion of a video that identifies the speaker or subject

M

mashup
a web application that combines information from one or more sources and presents it in a new way

microblog
a blog that consists of very short posts

mojo
mobile journalist; a journalist equipped with the equipment to report, produce, and/or broadcast a story while in the field

mov
a video file format for QuickTime movies

MP3
a compressed audio format

MP4
MPEG-4; a compressed multimedia file format

MPEG
a compressed video file format

multimedia
the use of two or more media such as text, audio, or video, to tell a story

MySpace
an online social network where users can interact with friends and create custom profile pages

N

natural sound
see *ambient sound*

nose room
see *lead room*

O

open source
software whose source code is publicly available for anyone to use, copy or modify

P

page views
the number of times a site or web page is accessed by an online visitor; also called *hits*

paginate
to divide online content and display it on separate web pages

pan
to move a video camera on a horizontal axis

PDF
Portable Document Format; a digital document format

photoblog
a blog comprised mainly of photos, often with very little text or commentary

Photoshop
a professional image-editing and computer graphics creation software; to digitally edit or alter an image or photograph

PHP
programming language used to create dynamic websites and online databases

PNG

Portable Network Graphics; a compressed image format

pixel
a tiny point of color that makes up a digital image

podcast
an audio or video series distributed over the internet for playback on a computer or portable audio player; the act of creating or distributing said recording

point-and-shoot
a photo or video camera that offers few or no manual controls

prosumer
a contraction of the words "professional" and "consumer" that signifies someone who falls in between these categories; a term that describes media equipment that is both easy to use and includes professional features

R

RAW
an uncompressed and unprocessed image format

resolution
the level of detail in a digital image

RSS
Really Simple Syndication; a system for distributing news and other regularly updated content

Ruby
programming language used to create online databases

S

search engine
online tool used for searching the web

search engine optimization (SEO)
the process of enhancing a website and/or its content to increase its rank in search engines

server
a computer that stores and "serves" files or data to other computers

shotgun
a directional microphone that is less sensitive to sound on its sides and rear

sidebar
in blogging, a column adjacent to the main posts or content

slideshow
a collection of photos with a similar theme displayed in sequence, often accompanied by short text captions

SLR
Single Lens Reflex; a camera in which the scene is viewed through the same lens that takes the picture

social bookmarking
the use of internet to save and share links to online content

social network
an online community where users communicate and interact with each other

soundbite
in video and audio, a short phrase or sentence that encapsulates a longer speech or interview

Soundslides
software used to produce Flash-based photo slideshows

storyboard
a sequence of images or drawings that details the plan for a video or multimedia story

streaming media
an audio or video file that is available for immediate listening or viewing without downloading

StumbleUpon
a social network site and search engine where users discover and rate websites, articles, photos and videos

stylesheet
a file that specifies the presentation or appearance of a website

T

tag
a word or phrase used to classify or categorize online content; to classify or categorize online content

talking head
in video, a shot of an interviewee that shows only his or her head and shoulders

thumbnail
a small version of a larger digital image

TIFF
Tagged Image File Format; a compressed image file format

tilt
to move a video camera up or down on a vertical axis

timeline
a visual representation of the sequence of audio and/or video clips in an editing program

traffic
on the web, the number or frequency of visitors to a web page or site

troll
a person who intentionally antagonizes other users of online discussion forums or message boards

Twitter
an online social network and microblogging site where users send and read other users' messages or "tweets"

U

URL
Uniform Resource Locator; the web address of a particular website, page or file

USB
Universal Serial Bus; a system for connecting a computer to external electronic equipment

username
a unique online identification or alias

V

videoblog
an ongoing series of videos either embedded in a blog or made available in chronological order; also called a *vlog*

viewfinder
a small, usually rectangular, opening in a camera used to compose an image

viral
term that describes online content that becomes quickly and unexpectedly popular as a result of being shared by many web users

vodcast
a video *podcast*

vlog
see *videoblog*

W

WAV
an uncompressed audio file format

waveform
a visual representation of an audio recording

Web 2.0
term used to describe online applications such as social networks and wikis that allow direct interaction between a website user and the site

web development
the process of creating, coding, or building a website or its

components, including online applications

white balance
a control on a digital camera used to adjust the color balance of the image; to use the color balancing feature

widget
a web element that can be embedded in a web page, blog, or social network profile

wiki
a website or application that allows online users to collaboratively author, edit, and modify information

WMA
Windows Media Audio; a digital audio format developed by Microsoft

X

XML
Extensible Markup Language; a computer language used to present data on the Web

XLR
a common three-pin connector system used to connect media equipment

Y

YouTube
a video sharing site and social network where users upload and share videos

Z

zoom
to focus a camera lens to obtain a closer or farther image

ABOUT THE AUTHOR

Mark S. Luckie is a digital journalist and founder of the multimedia journalism blog 10,000 Words, a popular online guide to trends in technical journalism. Mark has produced multimedia and interactive stories for The Washington Post, the Center for Investigative Reporting, *Entertainment Weekly*, *The Los Angeles Times*, *The Contra Costa Times*, and is a former crime and justice reporter for *The Daytona Beach News-Journal*. He is a graduate of the University of California at Berkeley School of Journalism where he received his master's in journalism and Bethune-Cookman College where he received bachelor's degrees in broadcast production and Spanish. Mark has served as a multimedia skills trainer for the Knight Digital Media Center and has lectured various collegiate groups and professional news organizations.